European Emigration
to the Americas,
1492 to Independence:
A Hemispheric View

EUROPEAN EMIGRATION TO THE AMERICAS, 1492 TO INDEPENDENCE: A HEMISPHERIC VIEW

by **Eric Hinderaker and Rebecca Horn**

Published by the
American Historical Association
400 A Street SE
Washington, DC 20003
www.historians.org

ABOUT THE AUTHORS

ERIC HINDERAKER, Distinguished Professor of History at the University of Utah, teaches courses on early North America. His scholarship focuses on relations between Europeans and Native Americans, the nature of early modern empires, and comparative colonization. He is the author of *Elusive Empires: Constructing Colonialism in the Ohio Valley, 1673–1800* (Cambridge University Press, 1997), *The Two Hendricks: Unraveling a Mohawk Mystery* (Harvard University Press, 2010), and *Boston's Massacre* (Harvard University Press, 2017).

REBECCA HORN teaches Latin American history at the University of Utah and served for almost ten years as the Director of the Center for Latin American Studies, a US Department of Education National Resource Center. Her scholarship concerns two fields—Nahua Studies and the comparative history of the early modern Americas. She is the author of *Postconquest Coyoacan: Nahua-Spanish Relations in Central Mexico, 1519–1650* (Stanford University Press, 1997), which concerns the history of indigenous Nahuatl-speaking peoples of central Mexico based on Spanish- and Nahuatl-language sources; and co-author of *Resilient Cultures: America's Native Peoples Confront European Colonization, 1500–1800*, 2nd ed. (Pearson, 2013).

Hinderaker and Horn are currently completing a book manuscript on the history of Spanish, Portuguese, British, and French America and the huge expanse of the Western Hemisphere that remained autonomous of European rule throughout the colonial period.

Published in 2020 by the American Historical Association. As publisher, the American Historical Association does not adopt official views on any field of history and does not necessarily agree or disagree with the views expressed in this book.

Cover Image: *A Dutch Hulk and a Boeier from The Sailing Vessels*, After Pieter Bruegel the Elder (Frans Huys and Cornelis Cort). The Metropolitan Museum of Art, Public Domain.

ISBN: 978-0-87229-287-1

Library of Congress Control Number: 202093284

TABLE OF CONTENTS

EUROPEAN EMIGRATION TO THE AMERICAS, 1492 TO INDEPENDENCE: A HEMISPHERIC VIEW

Euuropean colonization of the Americas was shaped by a massive relocation of European populations to American settings.[1] While this process can be seen as a single, widely differentiated but essentially coherent whole, most scholarship on the subject remains fragmented by countries of origin and American destinations. As a result, although implicit and explicit comparisons inform both scholarly and popular views of colonization, few accounts provide a hemispheric perspective on the process. In this essay, we seek to lay out the dominant patterns of migration in a broad sweep, considering all of the Americas and extending our analysis in time from 1492 until circa 1800, when most of the Americas were becoming independent of direct European rule.[2] The result is a synthetic essay that relies on the labor of many other historians of the early modern Americas, who have generated deep and complex literatures in several discrete fields.[3]

Everywhere Europeans arrived in the Americas, they settled among or dislocated Native American peoples. This transfer of populations was profoundly destructive to Native societies; it resulted in the repeated displacement and relocation of indigenous populations and often triggered further disruptions, as Native peoples nearer the coast were pushed inland into the interior. Moreover, European immigration to the Americas unfolded alongside the coerced, involuntary migration of millions of Africans to various settings throughout the Americas. While we deal directly in this essay with neither the displacement of Native American societies and appropriation of their lands nor the mass enslavement of Africans in American settings, both processes directly influenced the experiences of European migrants. The geographic spaces open to Europeans, the occupations they could pursue, and the opportunities they enjoyed were all inextricably tied to colonial violence and the patterns of appropriation and exploitation it enabled.[4]

Migration to the Americas unfolded in three long eras. During the sixteenth century, the *foundations* of colonial enterprise were laid, especially in the two great population centers of the Americas, where the Aztecs and Incas had already established thriving imperial regimes. The seventeenth century saw a dramatic *proliferation* of colonial sites, widespread *experimentation* with new labor regimes and patterns of social organization, and an *acceleration* of transatlantic immigration. By the eighteenth century the essential characteristics of the various colonies were becoming clear, and many regions experienced dramatic *growth* and *diversification* as emigrants responded to new transatlantic opportunities.

The traditional analytical categories of "push" and "pull" factors can be applied to some aspects of European migration streams in the early modern period. Poverty, lack of opportunity, and religious persecution set the stage for people to leave their homes, while certain American regions attracted more migrants than others. Mesoamerica and the Andes drew large numbers of Europeans a full century before any other region in the Americas, for example, and the gold rush in late colonial Brazil led to the migration of hundreds of thousands of Portuguese. Push-pull factors never remained static, as the economic, social, and political conditions in sending and receiving regions changed with time.

A push-pull framework, however, is in many ways an inadequate means to understanding European migration to the Americas in the early modern period. Many transatlantic migrants, for example, were temporary sojourners, neither pushed from a particular point of origin nor pulled to a singular destination but instead remaining on the move as they responded to opportunities or fulfilled their obligations. Royal officials and their retinues, merchants and their families, and soldiers fulfilling terms of service moved in ways that defied the logic of push and pull. Others moved more or less against their wills. Bound laborers, for example, often exercised little or no control, either over the decision to migrate or over their ultimate destinations. A push-pull paradigm that emphasizes individual choice therefore neglects the structural conditions that formed the broader context for migration. It also neglects such crucial elements as migration networks and migrants' gender, ethnicity, social status, life stage, even sibling position—all factors that helped to determine which individuals left and which stayed home.[5] Recent studies emphasize the many variables that affected individual experiences and highlight the variability and particularities of local and regional settings in Europe and in the Americas.

The attempt to estimate European rates of immigration to the Americas is filled with guesswork; the evidence for migration is patchy, and rates of return migration and death in transit are both subjects of conjecture. Nevertheless, we know enough to illuminate broad trends in European migration: sources, timing, and orders of magnitude. In all, it is likely that just over 2 million Europeans migrated to the Americas between 1492 and the end of the colonial period (see Table 1). More than half came from the Iberian Peninsula. Emigrants from Spain and Portugal together totaled more than 1.2 million, while those from the British Isles—England, Wales, Scotland, and Ireland—numbered nearly 0.75 million.[6] France contributed perhaps 100,000 individuals to overseas emigration counts (with an especially high rate of return migration), and the Netherlands about 25,000. Portugal, with a population estimated at 1.5 million at the beginning of the sixteenth century, sent the highest ratio of emigrants to domestic population; Britain—whose population was not more than 3 million—was not far behind. In contrast, France, Spain, and the Netherlands all experienced much lower rates of emigration as a percentage of the domestic population. At the beginning of the sixteenth century, France had a population estimated at about 15 million, Castile about 7 million, and the Low Countries about 2.5 million. (Indeed, as Ida Altman has noted, the most recent demographic analysis of Spain in the early modern era "virtually ignores emigration as a factor affecting population.")[7]

Table 1: European Migration to the Americas, 1492 to Independence[8]

Country of Origin		Estimate
Iberia	Spain	688,000
	Portugal	523,000
	Total	*1,211,000*
Britain	England	502,000
	Ireland	114,240
	Scotland	105,760
	Total	*722,000*
Germany/Switzerland		84,500
France		100,000
Netherlands		25,000
Total		*2,142,500*

Patterns of European migration evolved throughout the colonial era. The sixteenth century was dominated by Spain, which sent some quarter million emigrants to the Americas before any other European power had begun to establish itself as a demographic force across the Atlantic. The number of migrants picked up in the seventeenth century, at least until around 1650; at the same time, migrants from Portugal, England, Wales, and Ireland entered the Atlantic migration stream in large numbers, along with a smaller number from France, the Netherlands, and Scotland. In the eighteenth century, Spanish migration revived, and Portuguese migration boomed. Departures from England and Wales dropped off substantially, but the lure of emigration persisted in Scotland and Ireland and reached into the upper Rhine valley (present-day southern Germany and Switzerland) as well. In general, Europeans migrating to the Americas grew steadily more diverse as time went on. By the end of the colonial period, substantial numbers of immigrants had been drawn to the Americas from numerous regions of western Europe.

THE SIXTEENTH CENTURY

The first hundred years of European involvement in the Americas were dominated by Spanish initiative and focused on the geographical midpoint of the continents: first the net of islands spanning the eastern end of the Caribbean; then, quickly eclipsing them, the rich heartlands of the Aztec and Inca empires. More than a third of all Spanish migrants to the Americas arrived in the sixteenth century, before any other European power was involved in colonization in more than a glancing way, and their experiences shaped expectations for all the later colonial enterprises. Most Spanish migrants were attracted by the tremendous wealth of Mesoamerica and the Andes, conquered by Spain in the early sixteenth century, news of which traveled quickly.[9] About 243,000 Spaniards crossed the Atlantic in the sixteenth century, most bound for New Spain and Peru.[10]

Traditionally, historians have emphasized state regulation of emigration from Spain. In keeping with its desire to impose religious orthodoxy in the late fifteenth and early sixteenth centuries, the Spanish crown prohibited the passage of certain groups, including Protestants, Romanies, the Jews and Muslims forced to convert to Christianity and their descendants (known as New Christians, or *conversos* for Jews and *moriscos* for Muslims), and sometimes non-Spanish Europeans.[11] In 1503, the crown established the Casa de la Contratación (House of Trade) to oversee, along with transatlantic commerce, the licensing and departure of emigrants to its American territories. Each emigrant was to obtain both a royal license and proof of purity of blood (*limpieza de sangre*), typically acquired from local officials in the applicant's hometown. This cumbersome bureaucratic system, however, was not fully effective; many emigrants bypassed legal controls, and there are also significant gaps in the records.[12] Extant licenses thus fail to capture the full extent of Spanish emigration, even as historians use them, along with supporting documentation and the passenger lists from ships, to estimate overall numbers of emigrants.

The traditional focus on legal and institutional history tends to obscure the fact that most emigration from Spain was not directed by the crown but was privately organized and financed. In the earliest decades, emigrants came overwhelmingly from the south, especially the area around Seville, which enjoyed a monopoly on the American trade. After the conquests of Mexico and Peru, which dramatically enhanced the economic opportunities associated with emigration, the net was thrown wider to take in emigrants from throughout Castile, though female migrants continued to come disproportionately from Seville and its hinterland throughout the sixteenth century. Demographic, political, and economic push factors varied from place to place, producing substantial regional variation in emigration patterns.[13]

In the conquest years, most immigrants were men recruited to participate in expeditions that won Spain its territories.[14] As soon as the situation stabilized, however, women and children began to migrate; during the 1560s and 1570s, almost one-third of the immigrants were women. The presence of family groups also increased with time.[15] From the era of conquest onward, Spanish immigrants were drawn from every social and economic group in the middle ranks of Spanish society; only the very rich and very poor were notably underrepresented.[16] Unlike the rudimentary agricultural villages of New France, New England, and other parts of the Americas, the complex societies of Mesoamerica and the Andes could support a wide range of skills and employments from the beginning of colonization, and most Spaniards migrated to urban settings. Immigrants included royal officials, merchants, clerics, professionals, skilled artisans, and servants, among others, and they brought along or sent for their female relatives. By the mid-sixteenth century, male immigrants included mature adults already settled in their profession or trade, and most could expect to continue in their occupations in America.[17]

Men and women who were unable to obtain a license or purchase a passage sought help from friends or family or traveled as an employee or servant (*criado*) in the retinue of an official or wealthy patron. Such employment arrangements were informal, without the kind of written contract or specified length of service involved in the system of indentured servitude characteristic of French and British emigration a century later. *Criados* were drawn from diverse social groups and might serve for the duration of the journey, perhaps longer, though many struck out on their own once they arrived at their destination and found attractive opportunities. In sixteenth-century Mexico and Peru, Spaniards had no need to recruit bound European labor, as they relied on indigenous workers for unskilled tasks and Spanish *criados* and African slaves for those that required European skills or the supervision of indigenous people. In contrast to the French and English cases, Spanish emigrants were "remarkably free of legal obligations (such as labor contracts) that might restrict their liberty of movement and choice, although they were, of course, often influenced by continuing ties of patronage, kinship, or debt."[18]

Family and hometown ties structured transatlantic migration. Age, marital status, and position in the family often influenced who decided to leave or to stay. Sibling relations played a fundamental role in emigration, especially for women.[19] And in an extension of migration patterns within Spain itself, women of any social background rarely traveled alone to America.[20] Family members often supplied the financial resources for travel. Travelers relied on people from their hometowns who were resident in Seville to facilitate their stay there while they waited for a license to travel or made preparations to sail.[21] Most emigrants traveled with relatives, friends, or patrons, or left to join those already settled in America, from whom they anticipated help in getting established. Spaniards already in America sent recruitment letters home to Spain, many of them preserved among the applications for travel licenses.[22] These letters typically highlight opportunity and prosperity in America in contrast to Spain, a country "of so much misery and suffering that there is no future for anybody there," as one settler put it.[23]

Cycles and networks of emigration connected people and places in Spain and Spanish America.[24] A royal official or wholesale merchant promoted back to Spain after a stint in America might in turn send a younger relative, a son perhaps or a nephew, to the very place he had earlier served (indeed, the nephew was a central figure in the process of recruitment).[25] A family might send one or two recruits each generation, a pattern that continually renewed ties between particular Spanish and Spanish American communities. Relatives and townspeople followed earlier emigrants to particular destinations, and everywhere emigrants sought out relatives, friends, and people from their hometown or region. As Ida Altman and James Horn write: "Well over half of all emigrants from the Extremaduran cities of Trujillo and Cásceres went to Peru . . . and half of the emigrants to Chile in the seventeenth and eighteenth centuries were Basques."[26] In the sixty years after 1560, around a thousand emigrants left the textile-manufacturing town of Brihuega in Castile, most of them settling in Puebla, Mexico, the second most important city in New Spain.[27] These patterns of chain migration endured throughout the colonial period.

Return migration occurred, and although available sources do not allow reliable estimates, certain patterns are evident. In the early years, some Spanish women, especially widows, returned from the Caribbean islands, and some men who made fortunes in the conquest and early settlement of Mexico and Peru returned to enjoy their enormous wealth and elevated social status in Spain.[28] Others returned to petition the crown for privileges and rewards. Some men (typically unmarried) spent a stint in the Americas and returned to their hometowns with a modest stake to get reestablished; there they were known as *indianos*.[29] And some married men who had left their wives behind in Spain returned (either voluntarily or by force) after the crown, beginning in 1528, ordered them to rejoin their wives in Spain or to bring the women to them.[30] Return migration, Altman writes, "hinged on a number of factors, such as social and economic status, position within the family and timing of arrival in the Indies." Returnees might maintain ties or business dealings with people in the West Indies or local residents with connections there, at times intermarrying and establishing business relationships with one another, expanding family and friend networks and in the process reinforcing transatlantic connections as well as fostering subsequent emigration.[31] Return migration may have declined in the seventeenth century, when the crisis of the Spanish economy "discouraged return."[32]

Immigration to Spanish America was not limited to Spaniards. Royal restrictions notwithstanding, Europeans of diverse origins were everywhere. Before 1600, Portuguese and Italians traveled openly to Spanish America. Italians (especially Genoese) had been active in the Caribbean as merchants and financiers from the earliest years, though their presence diminished with time. Portuguese could be found throughout the sixteenth-century Caribbean and adjoining mainland areas. With time, they were present in Mexico, Venezuela, and the port cities of the Spanish empire, and especially in Peru, where they ventured up from the Río de la Plata region to gain access to the silver of Potosí.[33] The contraband trade they built also explains the strong Portuguese presence in the port city of Buenos Aires, where, "by the mid-seventeenth century they were by far the most numerous foreign element in the population . . . and were solidly entrenched both economically and socially." The union of Portugal and Spain (1580–1640) facilitated Portuguese immigration to Spanish America, while the Spanish *asiento*, which granted Portuguese merchants a monopoly to supply slaves to Spanish America, helped secure Portuguese power in Buenos Aires and elsewhere.[34] Many of the Portuguese resident in Spanish America were so-called New Christians, who in the sixteenth and seventeenth centuries created extensive social and commercial networks throughout the Atlantic world.[35]

Portugal had an American colony of its own in the sixteenth century, but at first it competed poorly with the opportunities available in either Spanish America or Portugal's far-flung African and Asian holdings. In Brazil, Portuguese mariners found no quick path to riches. The only immediately attractive resource was brazilwood, a dyewood the mariners acquired from local indigenous groups from the relative safety of their trading stations. Typically, those stations were located on easily defended islands along the coast, a pattern analogous to Portuguese enterprises in Africa. Though the brazilwood trade gave the Portuguese a foothold, it did little to inspire mass relocation.[36] In response to Brazil's failure to attract immigrants, the Portuguese crown turned to coerced or state-sponsored colonization. One such strategy involved sending convicted criminals, or *degredados*, into exile. In the colony's early decades, ship captains scattered *degredados* along newly charted coasts, in the hope that, should they survive, they would learn enough of the local languages to act as intermediaries later. Against all odds, this occasionally worked. The first large cargo of *degredados* arrived in 1549, along with the colony's first royal governor; throughout the sixteenth century, transported convicts made up a substantial portion of Brazil's Portuguese immigrant population. At the same time, the crown began to provide dowries to Portuguese women of marriageable age (known as "orphans of the king") who would resettle in Brazil. Yet, it was only when Portuguese fortunes declined in Asia and Brazil's sugar industry took off in the second half of the sixteenth century that Portuguese immigrants began to arrive in Brazil in significant numbers, settling largely in the northeastern sugar provinces of Bahia and Pernambuco. At century's end, Brazil had perhaps 30,000 European residents, and the growth of voluntary settlement was still in its earliest stages.[37]

In Spanish America, by contrast, a quarter million Europeans had crossed the Atlantic by the end of the sixteenth century, and the foundations of colonial society were firmly in place. The full range of Spanish immigrants was found only in Mexico and Peru, the first core areas of Spanish colonization. In the same period, more than 150,000 Africans were imported to Spanish America; again, most went to Mexico and Peru.[38] Peripheral regions—those places that lacked either sedentary indigenous populations or a viable export product—held little attraction for Spaniards, and few ventured there, especially in the sixteenth century. At times, Spanish authorities might directly sponsor or encourage immigration to those regions where private recruitment proved difficult, especially if strategic concerns were at stake. One example was the concession of Venezuela granted by Charles V to a German banking firm in 1528.[39] Yet, such crown initiatives, like Portuguese efforts to populate the Brazilian periphery with convicts and orphans of the king, only highlight the centrality of private enterprise, family networks, and individual initiative in laying the sixteenth-century foundations of European activity in the Americas. Wherever Europeans settled in large numbers in the centuries to come, these same forces shaped their efforts.

THE SEVENTEENTH CENTURY

Mesoamerica and the Andes offered an immediate field of opportunity to European emigrants. Elsewhere in the Americas, large-scale immigration was delayed less by the backwardness of Spain's European rivals than by the absence of opportunity and motive. By the opening decades of the seventeenth century, however, a host of new enterprises had begun to transform colonial landscapes. Sugar and tobacco production in Brazil, the Caribbean, and the Chesapeake drew the attention of investors and landowners and brought hundreds of thousands of laborers, most of them enslaved or bound by indentures, to do the backbreaking work those crops entailed. In northeastern North America, European-style agriculture, in combination with the fur and timber trades, the fishing industry, and Christian missions, drew smaller numbers of emigrants. To the south, the core regions of the Spanish empire continued to grow at the same time that Spaniards occupied strategically or economically valuable sites throughout South America and pushed north into New Mexico. During the seventeenth century, far-reaching economic and social experiments led to a proliferation of colonial sites and a dramatic increase in the number of migrants engaged in American enterprise.

The most important destinations, by far, for European emigrants in the seventeenth century were the sugar-producing regions of Brazil and the Caribbean. Though Brazil was the pioneer in this enterprise, and sugar made the colony a much more attractive destination than it had been in the brazilwood days, Portugal could not provide the labor necessary for the colony's success. It is difficult to detail migration patterns with confidence, because unlike Spain, which required emigrants to depart from a single official port and thus generated centralized records of departures, Portugal permitted departure from multiple ports both on the Iberian Peninsula and in the Azores. The earthquake of 1755 also destroyed much of the relevant documentation in Lisbon. With these constraints, historians estimate that another 70,000 or so Europeans emigrated to Brazil in the seventeenth century, for a total of about 100,000 emigrants between 1500 and 1700. The great majority were drawn to the colony's sugar-producing north, but they were far fewer in number than those traveling to either Spanish America or the sugar-producing islands of the Caribbean in the same period. Brazilian settlers were privately recruited and included people drawn from every rank of society by the hope of improving their circumstances. News of the Portuguese Atlantic was widely available; A. J. R. Russell-Wood remarks, "There must have been few villagers in Portugal who had not experienced the departure of a neighbor or relative or whose native sons had not sent news home."[40] These settlers did not expect to labor in the cane fields themselves, however, and only the large-scale importation of African slave labor made Brazil an attractive destination.

Most Portuguese immigrants to Brazil came from the Azores, the populous north of Portugal, or the port city of Lisbon and its hinterland.[41] Emigration from northern Portugal reflected the structural conditions of the economy; in much of the region, farmland was poor, holdings small, and poverty widespread. Lack of economic development or opportunity spurred a sustained pattern of emigration across three centuries of Portuguese expansion.[42] In the Azores, the conditions that fueled emigration similarly remained consistent across time—population pressure, chronic poverty, concentration of landholding, cycles of export economies, and even natural disasters, including earthquakes and volcanic eruptions.[43]

The extent of return migration from Brazil is difficult to estimate. Merchants, royal officials, and religious leaders were often temporary migrants. Successful mill owners and even *degredados* returned when they were able. As Brazil had no university, prominent families sent sons to Portugal for their education; daughters returned to secure a suitable marriage or entrance to a Portuguese convent. Close ties between Brazil and Portugal complicate the already difficult task to estimate the number of return migrants.[44]

As was so often the case in the American outposts of European empires, immigrants were disproportionately male throughout Brazil's colonial era, though the sex ratio gradually evened out through natural increase in established areas of settlement. The crown opposed creating a convent in Brazil well into the seventeenth century, for fear it would remove women of marriageable age from the population; even in the eighteenth century, Portuguese officials worried about a shortage of eligible European women. Nonetheless, the number of Portuguese women increased with time, so that "Portuguese-born women and their female offspring were present in sufficient numbers for there to be families who could count Portuguese descent on both sides over several generations."[45]

Portuguese immigrants to Brazil also included a large number of New Christians (*conversos*), the descendants of Jews forced to convert to Catholicism who fled from persecution in Portugal, especially after the Inquisition began there in the 1540s.[46] New Christians undertook many occupations, from plantation owner to artisan, but were especially prevalent as merchants. In this lattermost profession, their ties to relatives or co-religionists who had settled in the commercial cities of the Low Countries, above all Amsterdam, where they could live openly, proved advantageous.[47]

The growth of a viable economy brought other Europeans, including French, Spanish, Dutch, Italian, and English, to Brazil as well. Spanish immigration to Brazil gained additional encouragement from the union of the Spanish and Portuguese crowns between 1580 and 1640, while the Dutch occupation of northern Brazil (1630–54) brought many northern Europeans.[48] Most New Christians in Brazil were Portuguese, but some were of other nationalities too. During the era of Dutch occupation, Jews could live and practice their religion openly in Brazil, but many of those who came in the Dutch period left again when control of the colony reverted to Portugal.[49] Many Spaniards were counted among the *bandeirantes*, or participants in expeditions (*entradas*) setting out from São Paulo for the backlands in search of slaves and gold, a process that effectively opened up the Brazilian interior at century's end and set the stage for new directions of development in Brazil during the eighteenth century.[50]

As Brazil experienced its sugar revolution, English and French sailors and planters fanned out across much of the Caribbean. For decades they had used various islands as bases for raids against Spanish shipping. Then, beginning in 1624 with Saint Christopher (Saint Kitts), they established more permanent settlements. These new colonies—a dozen or so in all, including Saint Kitts, which was partitioned between English and French settlements; the French islands of Martinique, Guadeloupe, and Saint Barthélemy; and the English outposts of Nevis, Antigua, Montserrat, Anguilla, Tortola, and Barbados—experimented with unfamiliar foods like manioc and sweet potatoes at the same time that they attempted to cultivate a wide variety of cash crops, including tobacco, indigo, cotton, cacao, and ginger. Beginning around 1640, planters on many of the islands shifted to sugar cultivation. Where conditions were right, as they were in Nevis, Barbados, and Martinique, these colonies were soon producing substantial crops of sugar and, as a consequence, claimed some of the world's most valuable real estate.[51]

Eventually, the sugar islands of the English and French Caribbean would come to rely on enslaved African labor. But with no direct experience of slavery or contacts in the trade, English and French planters turned first to their own traditions of contract labor. In England such workers were called indentured servants; they agreed to labor for a period of years in exchange for "freedom dues" at the end of their terms of service, typically a period of four to seven years. The French *engagés* were much like English indentured servants except that their terms of service tended to be shorter—typically three years—and their employment conditions somewhat more favorable.[52]

Although England and France both employed contract labor in colonization, it operated in the two cases on entirely different scales. French merchants and ship captains relied on *engagés* to help manage their overseas ventures, but English colonies made contract labor the driving force in immigration from northern Europe in the colonial era. Scholars estimate that about 25 to 30 percent of the 2 million European emigrants to the Americas arrived under labor contracts.[53] Yet, more than half of those emigrants (approximately 1,211,000 people, or 60 percent of the total) originated in Spain and Portugal, where contract labor played no role in colonization. Of the remaining 816,000 emigrants, the majority embarked for the Americas from the British Isles, two-thirds to three-quarters under contracts of indenture.

In the earliest years of overseas colonization, servants from Britain performed essentially the same functions that African slaves did in Brazil. Hundreds of thousands of young men traveled under contract to places they often did not want to go. In many cases, these were destinations of last resort for people who had no other employment options. In the Americas they cleared tropical and semitropical landscapes, planted and tended sugarcane and tobacco, operated sugar mills in the withering heat of a Barbados summer, and cured and packed tobacco in Virginia and Maryland. After the transition to African slavery, conditions for indentured laborers in England's colonies gradually improved. But in the first half to three-quarters of the seventeenth century, before African slaves began to take their place, indentured servants performed the deadly work that laid the foundations of the sugar and tobacco plantations at the economic heart of England's transatlantic enterprise. Many failed even to survive the terms of their indentures, and very few prospered.[54]

More than 220,000 British emigrants traveled to the Caribbean, principally Barbados, in the seventeenth century. In 1655, an English fleet seized Jamaica from Spain; thereafter, Jamaica grew alongside Barbados as England's other most important sugar island. Emigration peaked between 1630 and 1660, when economic depression and civil war at home drove large numbers of Britons into overseas labor markets.[55] Most were indentured servants: young, single men of low social status, without work skills or employment prospects. An average of 2,000 migrants arrived in Barbados per year in the 1640s; the number rose to 3,000 per year in the early 1650s. Though the earliest migrants to Barbados hoped to complete short terms of service and become planters themselves, their dreams evaporated quickly. By the late 1640s, a majority of laborers transported to Barbados were convicts, rebels, or prisoners of war from Scotland, Ireland, and England, bound for as long as ten years and subjected to legal disabilities and forms of labor discipline unknown in the British Isles. Barbados planters "succeeded in fashioning a system in which servants were not free people contracted to work for others, but were instead a capital investment with many of the characteristics of property."[56]

Indentured labor also shaped the development of England's other staple-producing region. The semitropical climate of the Chesapeake was too temperate for sugar production but turned out to be ideal for growing tobacco. West Indian planters experimented with tobacco before shifting to sugar, and it was from the islands that John Rolfe first imported tobacco seeds to Virginia in 1614. Within a few years he had identified a commercially viable strain, and by 1619 the colony had shifted decisively to tobacco production. Like sugar, tobacco was a labor-intensive crop. From the time seeds were planted, just after Christmas, until the crop was harvested, dried, cured, and packed for shipping, a single season's harvest required fifteen months of steady labor. As in the sugar islands, indentured laborers were central to the developing tobacco economy of Virginia and, after 1625, Maryland.[57]

Most of these indentured servants embarked from the ports of southern England, but they came from all over England and Scotland, migrating to the urban centers of the southeast, often in stages, as they searched for work. Upon arrival in London or one of England's other port cities, they were prime candidates for overseas indentured labor. "In its earliest phase," as Bernard Bailyn puts it, "the peopling of North America was a spillover— an outgrowth, an extension—of . . . established patterns of mobility in England."[58] Ship captains recruited most of these indentured servants, especially in London and Bristol, and paid their passage in exchange for a period of labor servitude.[59] Irish Catholics joined the stream of migrants to the West Indies in the 1650s and 1660s, though it is difficult to say how many. Although Scots left their home country in large numbers in the latter half of the seventeenth century, only a few thousand indentured themselves to labor in Caribbean sugar plantations.[60]

During the seventeenth century, between 100,000 and 150,000 Britons migrated to the Chesapeake, 70–85 percent of them under labor contracts. As in the sugar islands, the region's supply of indentured labor was greatest around mid-century, when England's domestic economy was in dire condition. After 1660, rising wages and an improving economy in England made indentured servants scarcer and more expensive, and Scots began to outnumber English migrants. As the supply of servants shrank, those laborers who continued to go overseas generally preferred the Chesapeake to the islands as a destination, so servants remained available to Virginia and Maryland planters in substantial numbers into the 1680s, well after their Barbados counterparts had made a large-scale shift to enslaved African labor. However, after 1680 the dynamics of the British labor market shifted, and it became harder for Chesapeake planters to attract British laborers in numbers sufficient to their needs, and the importation of African slaves commenced in earnest.[61]

A minority of European migrants to the Chesapeake—some 15–30 percent—arrived without labor contracts. Like their indentured counterparts, these free migrants were predominantly single men embarking from southern and central England. In their middle to late twenties, they were a bit older than the servant population, which predominantly comprised men in their teens and early twenties. Though they did not typically travel in family groups, free migrants tended to have family ties to other free planters in the Chesapeake and to the merchant networks that handled the tobacco trade, and they maintained their transatlantic connections with letters and personal visits.[62] Some free migrants were barely better off than their bound counterparts but had been able to scrape together the cost of a transatlantic voyage; some were small merchants or middling landowners who were able to stake a modest sum on a Virginia trading house or plantation; and at the top of society was a very small, tightly interconnected cadre of gentleman landholders, government officials, and established merchants who together dominated the public life of the Chesapeake colonies.[63]

Though they made up a minority of the population, free emigrants shaped life in the Chesapeake colonies. Their initial investment in the tobacco economy was essential to the region's early development, as were their connections back home to the growth of commercial networks and the development of the colony's system of government. They also financed the transportation of most of the colony's indentured servants, a practice that became even more valuable to the colony's planters after the Virginia Company adopted the headright system in 1619. Under the terms of the headright policy, anyone who paid the passage of an emigrant to Virginia received title to fifty acres of land. Headrights became an important means for middling planters to increase their landholdings and rise in the ranks of Virginia society. For a lucky few enterprising souls, the opportunity afforded by the combination of tobacco planting and indentured servitude laid the foundation for substantial wealth.[64]

But the cards were stacked against most early migrants to the Chesapeake and the island colonies. Not only were the early immigrants overwhelmingly male, which made it hard for many to marry and form families, but the tropical and subtropical environments of these colonies exposed migrants from northern Europe to a host of unfamiliar pathogens. Like Native Americans encountering smallpox for the first time, Britons who confronted typhoid, dysentery, malaria, yellow fever, and other foreign maladies found them to be especially virulent. In Middlesex County, Virginia, high infant mortality produced a life expectancy of less than twenty years, which persisted throughout the seventeenth century. Even for those who survived until they were twenty, average life expectancy for women was only about forty years; for men, forty-five. By the time they reached adulthood, more than three-quarters of children born in the county had lost one parent and more than a third were orphaned. Only about a third of marriages in the seventeenth-century Chesapeake lasted as long as a decade; on average, a married couple could expect to bear only two children. All these things taken together—high rates of servitude, which delayed marriage and childbearing; an imbalanced sex ratio; high rates of disease and early death; and disrupted family structures—depressed fertility and dramatically slowed the growth of a native-born population. Virginians came to outnumber immigrants only around the end of the seventeenth century, ninety years after the colony's founding. Maryland's demographic history was similar. Though it is more difficult to gain precise estimates of Barbados's seventeenth-century population history, outcomes were almost certainly worse and were compounded there by higher rates of return migration.[65]

In its capacity to send hundreds of thousands of migrants to risky new lives in tropical and semitropical environments, England was unique. Its oversupply of population in the seventeenth century was unmatched by any other European country in the early modern period. In addition to its American emigrants, England sent some 180,000 people to Ireland in the seventeenth century. In all, it lost more than a half million people—perhaps 15 percent of its total population—to overseas emigration. The Netherlands and France also established sugar colonies during the seventeenth century, but neither sent large numbers of their own people to their Caribbean colonies. The Dutch Republic was a small federation with a far-reaching empire. Its most lucrative holdings were in Asia, and during the seventeenth and eighteenth centuries it sent more than 1 million emigrants—most of them from Germany, Scandinavia, and other parts of northern Europe—to the east. (The Netherlands themselves had a population of only about 2 million.) Though the Dutch established a half dozen colonies in the Caribbean, these served principally as bases of naval operations. The sugar plantations of Dutch Guiana depended from the beginning on enslaved African labor; the Dutch Republic never sent more than a trickle of emigrants to its Caribbean colonies.[66]

All told, Dutch colonies in the Americas received perhaps 25,000 European emigrants in the seventeenth century. The most important Dutch possessions in the Lesser Antilles were the islands of Sint Maarten (which the Dutch occupied jointly with the French after 1648), Curaçao, and Sint Eustatius. In addition, the Dutch occupied northeastern Brazil from 1630 to 1654 and conquered Suriname in 1667. All told, these tropical possessions attracted some 15,000 immigrants. In North America, New Netherland drew another 10,000 or so between its founding in 1614 and its conquest by the English in 1664. In all these locations, Dutch emigrants included a mix of free colonists, soldiers, and indentured servants. Many paid their own way; others were supported in their emigration by the Dutch West India Company, the city of Amsterdam, or the Van Rensselaer family. Most of these immigrants were male, and they included many foreigners. The Netherlands attracted migrants from all over Europe in the seventeenth century, and Dutch overseas migration, as Bernard Bailyn has noted, "was in large part a secondary distribution of recent arrivals," including half of those who arrived in New Netherland.[67]

Though the population of France—never less than 20 million during the seventeenth and eighteenth centuries—was vastly greater than that of either the Netherlands or Great Britain, scholars contend that fewer than 100,000 departed France for the Americas. Moreover, return migration from French colonies was especially high. Scholars disagree about the number of migrants to Canada—Leslie Choquette estimates up to 67,000 prior to 1763, while Mario Boleda argues for only 33,500, but both concur that net migration to Canada in the era of French colonization was about 20,000. Soldiers who were stationed in Canada were encouraged to remain, but only a small proportion did so; of the 4,577 soldiers who were sent to Canada between 1683 and 1727, for example, only about 20 percent stayed in the colony.[68]

Estimates of migration to the French West Indies and French Guiana are sketchier, but they suggest migration rates much lower than those of the English during the same era. In large part this is because most Frenchmen who migrated in search of work in the seventeenth century chose to travel south, to the Spanish countryside; only about 20 percent crossed the Atlantic. Of these, an estimated 75–80 percent went to the islands rather than New France. Jean Tanguy estimates that 30,000 to 40,000 *engagés* traveled from France to destinations in the Caribbean in the colonial era, most of them in the seventeenth century. Scholars agree that *engagé* migration dropped off dramatically after 1680, while an increasing number of African slaves were imported to meet the colonies' labor demand. French settlement in the Caribbean centered on the island colonies of Saint-Christophe, Martinique, Guadeloupe, and the western portion of the island of Hispaniola (which

Spain recognized as French territory in 1697 and the French came to call Saint-Domingue). Despite repeated efforts of colonial administrators, the colony of French Guiana on mainland South America remained tiny and underdeveloped by comparison. In 1670, some 15,000 Europeans lived in the French West Indies and Guiana, compared to 7,200 in French North America; by 1730, those numbers had risen to about 32,000 and 41,000 respectively.[69] Given these population figures, and assuming that death rates were comparable to those in other island colonies and return migration was similar to that from Canada, it seems likely that French migration to the Caribbean has been undercounted, but the data to support a revised estimate are unavailable.

Engagés were crucial to the development of France's colonies. About 39 percent of immigrants to New France were *engagés*, and their proportion in the Caribbean colonies was certainly higher. In one sample of 6,200 *engagés* who departed from La Rochelle, 80 percent were bound for the Caribbean.[70] *Engagés* were recruited privately, either by companies that oversaw settlement and trade or by individual planters, some of them former servants themselves. This form of direct recruitment meant that an individual agreeing to a labor contract often knew the identity of the master for whom he would work once he arrived in America—a contrast with the British system that drew laborers from a much wider territory under more anonymous circumstances. Most *engagés* were from urban areas, though not all; a good proportion had worked the land. Indentured servants were overwhelmingly single, young men; many of them followed relatives who had previously signed labor contracts.[71] They embarked from one of the French ports that specialized in the colonial trade—Le Havre was closely linked to Martinique, Dieppe to Guadeloupe. The numbers of indentured servants arriving in the French Caribbean fluctuated depending on the economy, wartime disruptions, and the demand for soldiers in France, among other factors.[72] After 1650, at the same time that African slaves began to enter the labor market in large numbers, recruitment became more speculative and anonymous. Working conditions deteriorated as a result, and the supply of *engagés* fell precipitously. By the end of the seventeenth century, the *engagé* system had fallen into disrepute among planters and prospective laborers alike. Only crown intervention would keep it alive in the eighteenth century.[73]

Despite the formal similarity between England's institution of indentured servitude and the French *engagé* system, they were used in very different ways. In the English system, indentured laborers exercised relatively little choice over the terms of their employment. In an era when the domestic economy simply could not absorb all its laborers, luckless young men streamed through London, Bristol, and a few other ports in search of a livelihood, however unpromising it may have been. In the colonies, their labor was hard and their lives were cheap. They were easily replaced. Some 360,000 of them made their way to the Caribbean or the Chesapeake during the seventeenth century; most died there without gaining independence or forming families. *Engagés* were used differently. Numbering only about 23,000 in France's Caribbean colonies, they were not simply strong backs to be thrown into field labor and used up until they expired. Only with the advent of African slavery did France's tropical colonies adopt the plantation model and begin to exploit their laborers in the brutal manner traditional to such enterprises. *Engagés* exercised choice and controlled their destinies in a way that indentured servants did not, at least not before the eighteenth century.

While the great majority of Britain's seventeenth-century emigrants traveled to tropical and semitropical destinations, often against their will, a relatively small trickle—perhaps 10 percent of the total—made their way to temperate colonies, where they sought to replicate, or at least approximate, European-style settlement and agriculture. In New England, as in Canada, colonists sought to create communities much like the ones they left behind. The environmental historian Alfred Crosby has labeled the regions that developed from these efforts "neo-Europes," to highlight the extent to which their complex of plant, animal, and human populations mirrored that of their parent societies.[74]

There were many similarities between the French colony of Canada (founded in 1608) and the English colonies of Plymouth (1620), Massachusetts Bay (1630), and Connecticut (1638). Each settlement combined European-style agriculture with an export economy based on the fur trade, the offshore fishing industry, and timbering. While none of these export commodities had the value or prestige of an exotic crop like sugar, taken together they kept their colonies afloat. In both Canada and New England, colonists created agricultural communities that replicated familiar models of social organization. These models differed from each other in important ways—the farming communities of Canada were designed as seigneuries that granted extensive privileges to noble or ecclesiastical grantees, while New England towns were based on freehold tenure—but each sought to recreate conditions essentially like those migrants would have known at home.[75]

New England and Canada attracted roughly comparable numbers of people in the seventeenth century. In the context of population flows elsewhere in the English Atlantic, the so-called Great Migration of

English Puritans seems misnamed. Perhaps 21,000 men, women, and children traveled to New England, principally to Massachusetts Bay, in the seventeenth century, nearly all of them between 1620 and 1633. This is less than 6 percent of the number who immigrated to the Caribbean and Chesapeake colonies. Net migration to Canada, as we have seen, numbered about 20,000 as well.[76]

Though the migrants to New England came in small numbers, their communities flourished. Plagued by none of the demographic problems afflicting colonies to the south—imbalanced sex ratios, unfavorable disease environments, contracts of indenture that delayed marriage, self-destructive communities dominated by young men on the make—the Puritans and other pilgrims of New England multiplied and prospered. By century's end, their numbers had quintupled, to about 100,000, while bachelorhood, early death, and return migration ensured that migrants to Virginia, Maryland, and Barbados did not come even close to maintaining their original numbers. In 1700, the population of the Chesapeake colonies (ca. 120,000) was barely greater than that of New England. Canada's population growth was much slower, thanks to high rates of return migration and a preponderance of male migrants over female. Canada never captured the French imagination as a desirable destination; by 1663, its population amounted to barely 3,500 colonists. Thereafter, improved recruitment strategies and natural increase contributed to steady, if not spectacular, growth. By 1763, when France ceded its territories east of the Mississippi to Great Britain, colonists there numbered 90,000.[77]

Late in the seventeenth century, several new temperate destinations opened to British settlement along the mid-Atlantic coast, expanding the zone of neo-European colonization. New Netherlands was captured by the English in 1664 and renamed New York. In 1674, James, the Duke of York, granted the province of New Jersey to two loyal supporters of England's royal family. Seven years later, in 1681, Charles II gave William Penn proprietary control over territory that would come to be called Pennsylvania. These new colonies were attractive destinations for tens of thousands of Britons, especially those of modest or middling means who wanted a new start. By century's end, they had attracted some 20,000 migrants, but their significance was only beginning to be felt. In contrast to the tropical and semitropical staple-producing colonies, where life was cheap and laboring conditions brutal, and to New England, where the emphasis on religious conformity dampened the interest of outsiders, these mid-Atlantic colonies developed a reputation as "the best poor man's country in the world." Whether free or indentured, migrants found opportunity of a kind that was not available elsewhere. Known as ethnically and religiously plural colonies, they became havens for Protestant sects that had been persecuted in Britain and on the European continent; they also became desirable destinations for thousands of migrants, both free and indentured, seeking independence and economic opportunity. As demand for indentured servants developed in the mid-Atlantic colonies, it grew correspondingly harder to attract them to colonies like Barbados and Virginia.[78]

While England, France, and the Netherlands made new forays into the Americas in the seventeenth century, Spanish America expanded in new directions as well. In the core regions of central Mexico and the Andes, peoples of European and mixed-race ancestry filled cities and countryside, and, at least in central Mexico, the indigenous population reached its nadir. Beyond the cores, complex patterns shaped demographic development. In South America, Buenos Aires, Bogotá, and Caracas, all founded in the sixteenth century, became increasingly important commercial centers as networks of smaller provincial towns, mining camps, haciendas, and plantations extended Spanish control farther into the hinterlands. Cacao, tobacco, cotton, and coffee plantations developed in the tropical valleys near the Caribbean coast, while in Colombia gold mining stimulated the growth of other new sources of wealth. Hispaniola, Cuba, and Puerto Rico remained strategically important in the Caribbean, but—in contrast to the French and English islands in the same era—were not yet being developed for intensive plantation agriculture. Beyond these secondary centers of development, mission settlements grew up in the seventeenth century across the far peripheries of Spanish America, among the Guaranís in Paraguay, the Pueblos in New Mexico, the Apalachees, Guales, and Timucuas in Florida, and other groups elsewhere.

Scholars estimate that roughly 195,000 Spaniards immigrated to the Americas in the first half of the seventeenth century—a rate of immigration higher than that of the entire sixteenth century, during which an estimated quarter million arrived. Although scholars generally accept the figure of a half million Spanish immigrants before 1650, the number that arrived afterward remains a matter of conjecture. Sources for the later period are less reliable than the license and ship registers from Seville, until 1668 the only official port for the American trade, from which the fleets departed. By the late seventeenth century, the fleet system was in total disarray, with irregular and unpredictable sailings, and more Spanish ports were permitted direct trade with the Americas. Scattered and inconsistent records thus make estimates of the number of Spanish immigrants hard to pin down, while at the same time fewer sailings meant a decline in actual opportunities for people to sail. Nicolás Sánchez-Albornoz considers it a "fair conjecture" that between

1650 and 1800, around a quarter million Spanish immigrants—less than half the number crossing before 1650—left Spain for the Americas.[79]

Patterns of Spanish immigration in the seventeenth century thus apparently carried forward from the sixteenth without radical change. Mexico in particular continued to appeal to immigrants, who settled there into a mature colonial society. In Mexico the indigenous population reached its nadir around the mid-seventeenth century, at which point modest recovery began; in Peru recovery began later, well into the eighteenth century. By 1650, the large-scale importation of African slaves to both regions had come to a halt, as other groups, including the increasing number of persons of mixed ancestry, filled the roles previously held by Africans. Although always a minority, the Spanish population grew with time, through both natural increase and immigration. In Mexico, immigrants claimed a declining proportion of this population (from 38 percent in 1570 to 8 percent in 1646 to 2 percent in 1742), integrating themselves into a context with an already established and increasingly dominant Creole population.[80]

Marked by the dramatic proliferation of new sites for occupation and settlement, diverse experiments in economic and social forms, and an astonishing flood of new migrants, especially from the British Isles, this era laid the demographic foundations for the transformation of the Americas. In the eighteenth century, the many new beginnings of this era of experimentation were extended and elaborated in a period of diversification and growth.

THE EIGHTEENTH CENTURY

The European migration to the Americas entered a new phase near the end of the seventeenth century. The proliferation and experimentation that marked the previous era gave way to a period in which immigration filled out established sites of colonization and spilled over to adjoining regions. European sources of immigrants shifted: immigration from the Netherlands, which had been inconsiderable in the seventeenth century, dried up altogether in the eighteenth. France continued to supply a steady trickle of immigrants, but its American destinations held no more appeal in the eighteenth century than they had in the seventeenth. Iberian immigration, which had continued throughout the seventeenth century (though exactly at what levels remains unclear), swelled again in response to new opportunities in both Brazil and Spanish America. The mainland colonies of Britain continued to attract a large number of indentured servants, alongside a burgeoning population of free migrants. Immigration from southern England held steady, while population flows from northern England, Scotland, Ireland, and the Rhine valley grew dramatically.

The Atlantic Ocean supported a much greater volume of sea traffic in the eighteenth century than it had in previous eras, which made immigration a more attractive and less chancy prospect than it had once been, especially for immigrants to British North America. Information about European labor supplies, opportunities for work, and the availability of land flowed more reliably and efficiently in both directions. While the core regions of New Spain had always exerted a strong pull on prospective migrants from Spain, large swaths of American territory now looked similarly appealing to many thousands of prospective emigrants in the British Isles and on the European continent. The same patterns of family and community recruitment and chain migration that structured immigration to New Spain in the sixteenth century and to New England in the seventeenth now shaped emigration from Ireland, Scotland, northern England, and the Rhine valley. Merchant firms with experience in transatlantic trade and migration also often facilitated decisions to emigrate. All these developments quickened the pace of immigration to the Americas.[81]

At the center of this process of economic expansion was the institution of African slavery. Enslaved Africans had been carried into American settings since the early sixteenth century, but African labor grew more concentrated in tropical and subtropical plantation settings in the second half of the seventeenth century, and the profitability of those plantation colonies exploded in the eighteenth. African slaves performed much of the hardest labor and generated products and profits that stimulated economic growth, which in turn created new opportunities for free migrants. In the eighteenth century, slaves worked the sugar plantations of Brazil and the Caribbean; the indigo and cacao plantations of Venezuela; the tobacco fields of the Chesapeake; the gold and diamond mines of Brazil; and the rice and indigo plantations of South Carolina and Georgia. These lucrative enterprises stimulated productivity and trade, and thus helped to drive a boom in labor demand and economic opportunity for Europeans in the fast-growing colonies of North and South America.[82]

Spanish immigration to the Americas in the eighteenth century picked up in response to the expansion of transatlantic commerce and the emergence of newly prosperous regions. Venezuela, New Granada, the Río de la Plata region, and the Spanish island colonies of the Caribbean all experienced dramatic demographic growth based on economic enterprises as diverse as gold mining; cacao, sugar, and tobacco production; and ranching. Immigrant origins shifted in the eighteenth century from the southern region of Iberia, especially Seville and its hinterland, dominant during the sixteenth and early seventeenth centuries, to the north and east, including Galicia, Asturias, the Basque region, and Catalonia. The Canary Islands also continued to be an important source of emigrants to the Americas in the eighteenth century.[83]

Many immigrants followed well-worn patterns of private sponsorship and initiative, traveling to the Americas to join family members or compatriots from the same hometown or region. Single young men still constituted a good portion of the migration stream.[84] Commonplace in the eighteenth century were the young men who sought business opportunities, often as employees of Creole merchants resident in Mexico City or Buenos Aires, both commercial cities that benefited from the economic prosperity of the late eighteenth century. These employees typically started out working in retail shops, competing with one another for promotion to clerk or even partner. Merchants often chose the most promising ones to marry their daughters, while their own sons trained for prestigious professional careers as clergy or government officials. Beyond his own talents, the immigrant son-in-law offered a merchant family renewed connections to commercial networks in Spain and the cachet of a peninsular marriage partner.[85]

State sponsorship of immigration, which had promoted settlement in peripheral regions of the empire from the earliest years of the sixteenth century, became more widespread in the eighteenth century. It served as one strategy in the attempt to shore up the defense of the empire, especially after the British captured and then occupied Havana for eleven months at the end of the Seven Years' War (1756–63). Full-time soldiers had been present in Spanish America over the centuries but in very limited numbers and capacities: as guards at viceregal courts and as soldiers at military forts (presidios) along the northern and southern Spanish American frontiers and at fortified ports in the Caribbean; elsewhere, the crown relied on civilian militias for defense against external enemies. With the more threatening circumstances of the eighteenth century, the crown for the first time dispatched large numbers of soldiers to the Americas. Between 1739 and 1798, an estimated 60,000 soldiers shipped across the Atlantic from Spain; most never returned. Some died, others deserted, yet others served out their contracts. Alongside soldiers, the crown sent prisoners (most of them military deserters) as laborers to strengthen and fortify Caribbean ports, especially Havana and San Juan. At the end of their terms, few prisoners actually returned to Spain, becoming, along with soldiers, a new element in the migration stream to eighteenth-century Spanish America.[86]

The crown also embarked on ambitious colonization schemes to populate vulnerable parts of the Caribbean, the northern Spanish borderlands, and the Río de la Plata region. These colonization efforts, which targeted family groups, also aimed to reduce population pressure in such places as Galicia and the Canary Islands. Indeed, for every 100 tons of merchandise, a ship leaving the Canary Islands was to carry five families. We know only the broad outlines of such eighteenth-century colonization projects, as the entire topic remains to be studied; even rough approximations are hard to come by. The crown paid passage for immigrants, who on arrival were to receive grants of land and supplies to establish agricultural communities. Some agricultural communities succeeded; others failed. When they failed, colonists rarely returned home; instead they sought opportunities elsewhere.[87]

With the discovery of gold in southern Brazil in the 1690s (and later diamonds), Portuguese immigration to the colony boomed in the eighteenth century. In addition to Portuguese colonists and African slaves migrating internally from the colony's north, hundreds of thousands of Portuguese immigrants streamed into the gold and diamond fields of southern Brazil; the Portuguese population in Brazil tripled in the 1700s. These immigrants were overwhelmingly young, single men; they came from the Azores, where population pressure was intensifying, and every region of mainland Portugal, but especially the densely populated north, and included "all social classes and occupations, from the peasantry to the gentry, including artisans, tradesmen, priests, and many with no fixed occupation."[88] Family and regional networks played a role. Brothers and nephews followed relatives who had migrated earlier; individuals likewise followed earlier emigrants from the same town or region.[89] Portugal numbered about 2 million people in 1700. Over the next century, an estimated 400,000 departed for Brazil, "despite efforts by the crown to place severe restrictions on emigration."[90] Portuguese migration to Brazil received a final boost near the end of the colonial period, when in 1808 the royal court fled the advancing Napoleonic armies by sailing to Brazil, along with as many as 15,000 people, including many nobles and royal, ecclesiastical, and military officials.[91]

Although the mining regions of Brazil attracted many immigrants in the eighteenth century, the Portuguese crown also turned to colonization projects to populate less desirable regions in both the north and south. The crown had already attempted this strategy earlier, in large part to protect its territorial claims from other Europeans. In the sixteenth century, the crown sponsored immigration to the northern coastal region in response to French competition for the brazilwood trade—the French port of Rouen was a major center of the trade—and attempts to establish settlements as potential refuges for French Protestants, or Huguenots.[92] In the seventeenth century, the crown again encouraged immigration to the region. Families from the

Azores and Madeira settled in Pará and Maranhão, among other locations along the coast. In the eighteenth century, the crown pursued sponsored colonization yet more forcefully, channeling families "particularly from the impoverished and overpopulated Atlantic islands . . . directly to vulnerable coastal areas or to disputed frontier regions," including Santa Catalina and Rio Grande do Sul in the south and Pará and Maranhão in the north. The crown continued this policy even into the nineteenth century, when in 1808 it provided families from the Azores and Madeira financial incentives, land, and supplies—and in 1813 exemption from military service—to relocate to Brazil, not only to the south but other regions as well.[93]

The mainland colonies of British North America received two great waves of non-English European migrants beginning in the second decade of the eighteenth century. In both cases, strong push factors worked to displace these populations, but increasingly powerful pull factors drew them to North America and particularly to Pennsylvania. The first came from Ireland, where Scots who had been recruited to work on English estates—the so-called Scots-Irish—began to emigrate in large numbers in 1718. As Presbyterians in Anglican communities, they had long been excluded by test oaths from political participation; in the second decade of the eighteenth century, economic hardships coincided with dramatic rent increases to begin pushing waves of Scots-Irish migrants across the Atlantic. The first phase of Scots-Irish migration, which began in 1718 and crested in 1729, brought several thousand migrants to Pennsylvania. Their experience was sufficiently favorable that many more followed. By 1780, about 114,000 people had emigrated from Ireland. A small number were Irish Catholic, but the large majority were Scottish and Presbyterian.[94]

At almost the same time, Protestants in the Rhine valley were displaced in enormous numbers by a similar combination of forces: religious discrimination coupled with economic dislocation. The result was a mass exodus of some 800,000 people from the upper Rhine in the eighteenth century. Most moved north and east to more hospitable European sites, but a minority undertook the arduous journey down the Rhine to Rotterdam, where they boarded ships that carried them to North America; almost all of them disembarked in Philadelphia. By 1775, an estimated 84,500 German-speaking people had immigrated to North America, about three-quarters of them to Pennsylvania. Along with the colony's growing English population, these Scots-Irish and German immigrants first helped to pioneer central Pennsylvania and then, beginning in the 1730s, pushed southward down the Shenandoah Valley of western Virginia as far as the Carolina piedmont. By the late eighteenth century, the western edge of colonial occupation in Pennsylvania, Maryland, Virginia, and North and

South Carolina had developed a distinct identity as the mid-Atlantic "backcountry."[95]

England, Wales, and Scotland also continued to supply a steady stream of migrants in the eighteenth century that, taken together, probably numbered just over 100,000 people. By the 1770s, two distinct patterns shaped this migration. The first pattern involved migrants from southern England, including London, Bristol, and the home counties, who were predominantly male indentured servants. They were not, however, the very young, unskilled laborers of the seventeenth century; a large majority were tradesmen or craftsmen who used contracts of indenture to pay their way across the Atlantic, but who often had considerable control over their destinations and employments in America. They committed to the voyage in response to good information about the demand for skilled labor. Demand was, in fact, high in many occupations, especially in the iron industry and the building trades. Most indentured servants went to Pennsylvania, Maryland, and Virginia: colonies at the geographical heart of British North America, which were experiencing dramatic growth and expansion during the eighteenth century. Convict labor constituted a distinct subset of this indentured population. From its establishment until 1775, the so-called Transportation Act of 1718 allowed British judges to commute capital sentences and send convicts across the ocean rather than to the gallows. Under the terms of the act, some 50,000 convicts joined the broader stream of indentured servants. The convicts too were predominantly young and male, and most ended up in the Chesapeake colonies of Virginia and Maryland. They were, however, especially likely to be unskilled; that fact, combined with their convict status, meant that their contracts were cheaper and their terms of service longer that those of other servants. Nevertheless, for the most part they were indistinguishable from the larger servant population once they arrived in North America.[96]

The second pattern of British emigration in the eighteenth century looked very different from the first. It originated in the north of England and Scotland and brought entire families rather than single laborers to North America. And rather than disembarking near the geographical midpoint of Britain's American colonies, where lands were largely occupied but labor was in high demand, they tended to travel to the peripheries, where colony officials, investors, and speculators were making new agricultural lands available to prospective settlers. After 1763, Nova Scotia and Florida were especially important destinations, but pockets of land became available in many places during the course of the eighteenth century, and many British farm families crossed the Atlantic with the intention of gaining a measure of independence in North America.[97]

In contrast to Iberian and British America, France's American colonies continued to struggle demographically. The Caribbean colonies attracted few voluntary newcomers. Hoping to bolster the European population of the islands, in part to aid in their defense against incursions by the English and Dutch, the French crown in 1698 obliged ships to carry a certain number of servants in proportion to their tonnage. This policy caused a major rift, deepening in the eighteenth century, between the crown and the planters, merchants, and ship captains who saw little benefit in continuing what they considered an out-of-date system. They complained about the difficulty of meeting the requirements, and with diminished demand, expressed the fear that workers might "go off to swell the mobile ranks of vagabonds, pirates, or buccaneers." Fraud was rampant; ship captains did everything they could to avoid compliance. The crown periodically suspended the requirement, especially in wartime, when the recruitment of soldiers took priority. In 1774, it abandoned the policy altogether.[98]

France's mainland colonies fared no better. New France comprised five distinct regions of settlement by the eighteenth century: Canada (the modern province of Quebec), Acadia (modern Nova Scotia), Île Royal (Cape Breton), the Illinois country, and Louisiana. After 1700, the colony experienced a small increase in the immigration of men of means, including planters, merchants, and government officials, but for the most part French men and women were unwilling to go to New France on their own initiative and at their own expense. Most arrivals came as indentured servants, soldiers, or prisoners. A crown policy that sent convicts to labor in Louisiana helped to address the colony's pressing need for workers but at the same time damaged its reputation among prospective free migrants. Throughout the seventeenth and eighteenth centuries, an estimated two-thirds of immigrants to New France returned to Europe at the expiration of their terms of service. By the end of the French period, Louisiana had a population of perhaps 4,000 Europeans, and the Illinois country another 1,500. Thus, one historian of Canada has concluded, the "inability to attract—and to keep—substantial numbers of immigrants" largely characterized New France.[99]

Two demographic catastrophes punctuated French experience in the Americas in the eighteenth century. The expulsion of French colonists from Acadia after its conquest by the British in 1755 set off a three-decade-long diaspora that carried thousands of colonists to various destinations in mainland North and South America, the Caribbean, the Falkland Islands, and France itself. In one destination after another, French imperial administrators hoped to use the ready-made population of Acadians to supply the muscle power for new colonizing initiatives; in every case, the venture failed more or less spectacularly. A couple hundred Acadians were recruited to the most egregious of these failures: the Kourou colony in French Guiana. Conceived as an experiment in Enlightenment social engineering and intended to "console the nation for the loss of Canada," Kourou instead became a graveyard for thousands of prospective colonists. Beginning in 1763, some 17,000 people made their way to ports of embarkation to participate in the Kourou expedition, among them approximately 11,500 German speakers from Alsace and the Rhineland. Of those 17,000, some 13,000–14,000 sailed for Guiana. The tiny settlement on the Kourou River was incapable of absorbing so many newcomers so quickly, and within a few months, 9,000 had died from starvation and tropical diseases. Perhaps 3,000 returned to France, but many of the returnees soon died as well.[100] The Kourou disaster highlights the extent to which, even in the late eighteenth century, the French experience in transatlantic migration stands as a striking counterpart to that of Spain, Portugal, and Britain.

CONCLUSIONS

What are the essential outlines of this long, complex pattern of migration and resettlement? To begin with, the Iberian roots of European immigration to the Americas should not be forgotten: for a century prior to the beginning of large-scale immigration elsewhere, the core regions of Spanish and, to a lesser degree, Portuguese colonization drew Europeans by the hundreds of thousands. This sixteenth-century pattern anticipated the seventeenth- and eighteenth-century proliferation of European departures and American arrivals. And despite the widely held notion that immigration to Spanish colonies was controlled and directed by the crown, while British immigration was the result of private initiative, it is abundantly clear that, everywhere in the Americas, immigration was driven forward by private motives, initiatives, and capital. State sponsorship of immigration, often accompanied by various forms of coercion, was nearly always undertaken to overcome the lack of interest in marginal places—and it nearly always failed to make a difference. Wherever Europeans immigrated in large numbers, they did so on their own initiative, in defiance of crown policies when necessary.

If opportunities in the core regions of Spanish colonization drove the first great wave of Iberian emigration, demand for labor in the plantation colonies of the Caribbean and the Chesapeake triggered the first wave of mass immigration from the British Isles. Plantation colonies created enormous labor demand wherever they were founded, but only in England's colonies did large numbers of Europeans fulfill that demand prior to the shift to African slavery. In contrast to France and the Netherlands, England had both a large surplus population and an institution—indentured servitude—that, like chattel slavery, could be adapted to fill a very large demand for coerced labor. While young men nearly always predominated in early migrant groups, the most striking difference in the experiences of European migrants related to the use of labor contracts to organize overseas migration. Such contracts were pervasive in Britain, common in France, but almost unheard of in Spain and Portugal. And only in Britain did they lay the foundation for a mass migration of unfree labor.

As the European colonies in the Americas matured, zones of primary production—those regions that produced silver, gold, and staple crops that were highly valued at home—created ever-expanding spheres of opportunity in zones of secondary production. Those opportunities, in turn, drew hundreds of thousands of migrants beginning in the late seventeenth century and continuing throughout the eighteenth. At the same time, more than any other colonized region of the Americas, the core regions of Spanish America—Peru and, especially, central Mexico—acted more or less continuously as a magnet for European immigration. As home to the two great indigenous empires of the Americas prior to contact, they were unique in the hemisphere. After the conquest, they offered a range and depth of economic opportunity that could not be found anywhere else in the Americas, at least until the eighteenth century.

Three great demographic transformations, each driven by European colonization of the Americas, reshaped the Western Hemisphere in the early modern era. One was the vast demographic catastrophe visited upon Native American populations by the violence, exploitation, and displacements of the colonial encounter. The second was the mass transport of some 12 million enslaved Africans across the Atlantic to labor in American settings. Both of these transformations have been treated by numerous scholars in their broadest outlines and are understood as hemisphere-wide phenomena. The third transformation came as a result of the immigration of some 2 million Europeans into American settings. This essay seeks to clarify broad patterns in that third transformation and to understand it, too, as a hemisphere-wide phenomenon. We demonstrate that the Spanish, Portuguese, and British empires, in particular, shared in common the capacity to transport astonishingly large numbers of Europeans across the Atlantic over a very long period of time. Alongside the demographic collapse of Native American populations and the trade in enslaved Africans, this phenomenon is the third element in the demographic transformation of the Americas in the early modern era.

ENDNOTES

1. The authors wish to thank the anonymous reviewers of this essay, and also Ida Altman and Aaron Fogleman, for their helpful comments and suggestions.

2. This essay ends with independence because migration patterns shifted dramatically afterward, and independence arrived at different times in each of the empires under consideration. For British North America, the end point of our data and analysis is 1783 (though some data sets use 1775 or 1776 as their cutoff); for Spanish America, our data and analysis include migrants in the first two decades of the nineteenth century, though European wars caused migration levels to drop precipitously in that period. On the dramatic changes in migration after independence, see Aaron Spencer Fogleman, "The United States and the Transformation of Transatlantic Migration during the Age of Revolution and Emancipation," in *The American Revolution Reborn*, ed. Patrick Spero and Michael Zuckerman (Philadelphia: University of Pennsylvania Press, 2016), 251–69. Similarly, the century-by-century analysis presented here is broadly accurate, but appropriate cutoff dates vary from empire to empire. Readers should understand that the data and analysis presented here are necessarily imprecise in their periodization.

3. For excellent, succinct introductions to the comparative history of European immigration to the Americas in the early modern period, see Ida Altman and James Horn, introduction, in Ida Altman and James Horn, eds., *"To Make America": European Migration in the Early Modern Period* (Berkeley: University of California Press, 1991), 1–29; and Nicholas Canny, "In Search of a Better Home? European Overseas Migration, 1500–1800," in Nicholas Canny, ed., *Europeans on the Move: Studies on European Migration, 1500–1800* (Oxford: Clarendon Press, 1994), 263–83 and following bibliography. We have elsewhere made a case for treating the colonization of the Americas as a single, highly differentiated but fundamentally unified process; see Eric Hinderaker and Rebecca Horn, "Territorial Crossings: Histories and Historiographies of the Early Americas," *William and Mary Quarterly*, 3rd ser. [henceforth *WMQ*] (67), July 2010, 395–432.

4. The relationship among colonial immigration, Native displacement and depopulation, and African exploitation is highlighted in Ida Altman,

"Migration and Mobility in the Sixteenth-Century Hispanic World," *Renaissance Quarterly* 67 (2014), 544–52.

5. For a discussion of shifting theoretical approaches to migration, see Dick Hoerder, *Cultures in Contact: World Migrations in the Second Millennium* (Durham, NC, and London: Duke University Press, 2002), 8–21.

6. Because historians often lump together the British kingdoms but separate the Iberian ones, it is common to say that Britain contributed the largest number of American emigrants in these years, with Spain second and Portugal third. But it is as problematic to treat Britain as a single political, social, or cultural entity in this period as it is to treat Spain and Portugal that way. Emigrants came from England, Wales, Scotland, and Ireland in large numbers; they migrated under the auspices of two crowns and three parliaments in the seventeenth century and belonged to four distinct language groups. Only after 1707 were England and Scotland formally united under a single crown. It is true that migrants from throughout the British Isles generally migrated to English-controlled colonies, while Spain and Portugal each controlled distinct territories. But the crowns of Spain and Portugal were united from 1580 to 1640; in that era, especially, Spanish and Portuguese migrants often shared destinations.

7. These European population estimates from ca. 1500 come from Felipe Fernández-Armesto, "Portuguese Expansion in a Global Context," in Francisco Bethencourt and Diogo Ramada Curto, eds., *Portuguese Oceanic Expansion, 1400–1800* (New York: Cambridge University Press, 2007), 484n8; but for the Netherlands, see also Jan Lucassen, "The Netherlands, the Dutch, and Long-Distance Migration in the Late Sixteenth to Early Nineteenth Centuries," in Canny, ed., *Europeans on the Move*, 153–91, who estimates 1.5–2 million. Ida Altman, "A New World in the Old: Local Society and Spanish Emigration to the Indies," in Altman and Horn, eds., *"To Make America"*, 33.

8. For Spain, see Magnus Mörner, "Spanish Migration to the New World prior to 1810: A Report on the State of Research," in Fred Chiappelli, ed., *First Images of America: The Impact of the New World on the Old* (Berkeley and Los Angeles: University of California Press, 1976), 2:737–82; Nicolás Sánchez-Albornoz, "The First Transatlantic Transfer: Spanish Migration to the New World, 1493–1810," in Canny, ed., *Europeans on the Move*, 32–33; and n. 79, below. For Portugal, see Stanley L. Engerman and Kenneth L. Sokoloff, "Factor Endowments, Institutions, and Differential Paths of Growth among New World Economies: A View from Economic Historians of the United States," in Stephen Haber, ed., *How Latin America Fell Behind:*

Essays on the Economic Histories of Brazil and Mexico, 1800–1914 (Stanford, CA: Stanford University Press, 1997), table 10.1, p. 264; this estimate includes the eighteenth century only until 1760. For Britain, we have followed Altman and Horn, introduction, in Altman and Horn, eds., *"To Make America"*, table 1.1, p. 3, which provides estimates for 1607–1780; see also Henry Gemery, "Emigration from the British Isles to the New World, 1630–1700: Inferences from Colonial Populations," *Research in Economic History* 5 (1980), 179–231, who estimates a total British emigration of 702,500–724,500 between 1630 and 1790; and Engerman and Sokoloff, "Factor Endowments," in Haber, ed., *How Latin America Fell Behind*, table 10.1, p. 264, who estimate a total of 746,000 emigrants between 1580 and 1760. Compare to the essays in Canny, ed., *Europeans on the Move*: Nicholas Canny, "English Migration into and across the Atlantic during the Seventeenth and Eighteenth Centuries," table 4.1, p. 64, presents the unusually low estimate of 420,500 English migrants to the Americas, as a consequence of positing a higher level of English migration to Ireland in the seventeenth and eighteenth centuries than is usually allowed; T. C. Smout, N. C. Landsman, and T. M. Devine, "Scottish Emigration in the Seventeenth and Eighteenth Centuries," tables 5.2, 5.3, and 5.4, pp. 90, 98, and 104, estimate 88,000 Scots emigrating to the Americas from 1650 to 1800; and L. M. Cullen, "The Irish Diaspora of the Seventeenth and Eighteenth Centuries," tables 6.1 and 6.2, pp. 139–40, posits 95,000 Irish migrants from 1600 to 1783. Altman and Horn estimate that Scotland and Ireland together contributed 190,000–250,000 emigrants to Britain's total; we have used the midpoint of that range—220,000—and pushed the estimates from Smout et al. and Cullen upward proportionally to reach that number. The number for Wales is included in that for England. For Germany and Switzerland, we follow Aaron Fogleman's estimate to 1775 in *Hopeful Journeys: German Immigration, Settlement, and Political Culture in Colonial America, 1717–1775* (Philadelphia: University of Pennsylvania Press, 1996), table 1.1, p. 2; for the last quarter of the eighteenth century, see Georg Fertig, "Transatlantic Migration from the German-Speaking Parts of Central Europe, 1600–1800: Proportions, Structures, and Explanations," in Canny, ed., *Europeans on the Move*, 202, who estimates a total of 100,000 German-speaking migrants by 1800. For France, we have chosen the high end of the range normally identified by historians, based on our view that migrants to Caribbean destinations have likely been undercounted; see n. 68 and n. 69, below. For the Netherlands, see Lucassen, "The Netherlands, the Dutch, and Long-Distance Migration," in Canny, ed., *Europeans on the Move*, 153–91. All these numbers are subject to debate; Altman and Horn, introduction, in Altman and Horn, eds., *"To Make America"*, 3, estimate a total European migration to the Americas of 1.5 million.

9. On Spanish immigration to the Americas, see the articles by Woodrow Borah, Peter Boyd-Bowman, James Lockhart, and Magnus Mörner (the last with an accompanying bibliography), in Chiappelli, ed., *First Images of America*, vol. 2; Peter Boyd-Bowman, "Patterns of Spanish Emigration to the Indies until 1600," *Hispanic American Historical Review* [henceforth *HAHR*] 56:4 (1976), 580–604; Nicolás Sánchez-Albornoz, "The Population of Colonial Spanish America," in Leslie Bethell, ed., *The Cambridge History of Latin America* [henceforth *CHLA*], 11 vols. (Cambridge: Cambridge University Press, 1984–95), 2:3–35; Sánchez-Albornoz, "The First Transatlantic Transfer," in Canny, ed., *Europeans on the Move*, 26–36; Magnus Mörner, "Migraciones a Hispanoamérica durante la época colonial," *Anuario de estudios americanos* (Seville), supplement, 48:2 (1991), 3–25; Altman, "A New World in the Old," in Altman and Horn, eds., *"To Make America"*, 30–58; and Ida Altman, "Moving Around and Moving On: Spanish Emigration in the Sixteenth Century," in Jan Lucassen and Leo Lucassen, eds., *Migration, Migration History, History: Old Paradigms and New Perspectives* (Bern: Peter Lang, 1997), 253–69; and Hoerder, *Cultures in Contact*, 191–94.

10. Magnus Mörner estimates roughly 243,000 emigrants in the sixteenth century, a figure that has been widely accepted in the field. See Mörner, "Spanish Migration to the New World prior to 1810," in Chiappelli, ed., *First Images of America*, 2:737–82.

11. On the legal exclusion of foreigners from Spanish America, see Sánchez-Albornoz, "The First Transatlantic Transfer," in Canny, ed., *Europeans on the Move*, 29. For a brief period (1526–38), Holy Roman Emperor Charles V permitted foreign subjects to emigrate. See Mörner, "Spanish Migration to the New World prior to 1810," in Chiappelli, ed., *First Images of America*, 2:738.

12. On bureaucratic procedures to emigrate from Spain, see Auke Pieter Jacobs, "Legal and Illegal Immigration from Seville, 1550–1650," in Altman and Horn, eds., *"To Make America"*, 59–84. Jacobs argues that many emigrants traveled illegally, with fraudulent documents or the complicity of lenient officials, even in some cases as stowaways. Sailors (many of them non-Spanish) at times deserted once they arrived in port. And every emigrant did not necessarily have a separate license, including servants traveling with royal officials or dependent members of households. Many non-Spanish Europeans may also have claimed to be natives of Hapsburg territories outside of Spain or may have received naturalization papers that

identified them as Spaniards. Also see Auke Pieter Jacobs, "Pasajeros y polizones: Algunas observaciones sobre la emigración española a las Indias durante el siglo XVI," *Revista de Indias* (Seville) 43 (1983), 439–79; and Auke Pieter Jacobs, "Las migraciones españolas a América dentro de una perspectiva europea, 1500–1700," in Jan Lechner, ed., *España y Holanda* (Amsterdam: Rodopi, 1995), 243–64. For Muslims and *moriscos* who evaded prohibitions and emigrated to Spanish America, see Karoline P. Cook, *Forbidden Passages: Muslims and Moriscos in Colonial Spanish America* (Philadelphia: University of Pennsylvania Press, 2016). The Canary Islands also served as a waystation for ships heading to the Indies. In addition to supplies, ships often took on soldiers or sailors, or other passengers without authorization to sail, including Canary Islanders or people deliberately avoiding the official emigration controls in Seville; see James Parsons, "The Migration of Canary Islanders to the Americas: An Unbroken Current since Columbus," *The Americas* 39:4 (1983), 447–81.

13. James Lockhart and Stuart Schwartz, *Early Latin America: A History of Colonial Spanish America and Brazil* (Cambridge: Cambridge University Press, 1983), 65; Mörner, "Spanish Migration to the New World prior to 1810," in Chiappelli, ed., *First Images of America*, 2:746; Altman, "Moving Around and Moving On," in Lucassen and Lucassen, eds., *Migration, Migration History, History*, 259–60; Ida Altman, "Spanish Migration to the Americas," in Robin Cohen, ed., *The Cambridge Survey of World Migration* (Cambridge: Cambridge University Press, 1995), 28–32; Carla Rahn Phillips, "Time and Duration: A Model for the Economy of Early Modern Spain," *American Historical Review* 92:3 (1987), 531–62; Altman and Horn, introduction, in Altman and Horn, eds., *"To Make America"*, 4.

14. Boyd-Bowman, "Patterns of Spanish Emigration," *HAHR*, 582; James Lockhart, *The Men of Cajamarca: A Social and Biographical Study of the First Conquerors of Peru* (Austin: University of Texas Press, 1972); John E. Kicza, "Patterns in Early Spanish Overseas Expansion," *WMQ* 49 (1992), 247–48.

15. Boyd-Bowman, "Patterns of Spanish Emigration," *HAHR*, 583. By this time, Boyd-Bowman tells us, "new decrees had made it illegal for a married man to emigrate without his wife or to remain in the colonies without sending for her," although often these orders were not observed. On Spanish women emigrants, see Ida Altman, "Marriage, Family, and Ethnicity in the Early Spanish Caribbean," *WMQ* 70 (2013), 225–50; Ida Altman, "Spanish Women in the Caribbean, 1493–1540," in Sarah E. Owens and Jane E. Mangan, eds., *Women of the Iberian Atlantic* (Baton Rouge: Louisiana State University Press, 2012), 49–67; and Ida Altman,

"Spanish Women and the Indies: Transatlantic Migration in the Early Modern Period," in M. Anore Horton, ed., *New Perspectives on Women and Migration in Colonial Latin America* (Princeton, NJ: The Program in Latin American Studies, Princeton University, 2001), 21–45.

16. Altman, "A New World in the Old," in Altman and Horn, eds., *"To Make America"*, 36. Even the conquest expeditions included men from a broad range of social backgrounds; see, e.g., Lockhart, *The Men of Cajamarca*; Kicza, "Patterns in Early Spanish Overseas Expansion," *WMQ*, 247–48; Matthew Restall, *Seven Myths of the Spanish Conquest* (Oxford: Oxford University Press, 2003), 27–43.

17. Boyd-Bowman, "Patterns of Spanish Emigration," *HAHR*, 583.

18. On *criados*, see Sánchez-Albornoz, "The First Transatlantic Transfer," in Canny, ed., *Europeans on the Move*, 30; Altman, "Spanish Migration to the Americas," in Cohen, ed., *The Cambridge Survey of World Migration*, 29; Altman, "Spanish Women and the Indies," in Horton, ed., *New Perspectives on Women*, 24–27; Altman and Horn, introduction, in Altman and Horn, eds., *"To Make America"*, 7, 14–15, quotation: 15.

19. Amelia Almorza Hidalgo, "Sibling Relations in Spanish Emigration to Latin America, 1520–1620," *European Review of History* 17:5 (2010), 735–52.

20. Altman, "Moving Around and Moving On," in Lucassen and Lucassen, eds., *Migration, Migration History, History*, 258–60.

21. Altman, "Moving Around and Moving On," in Lucassen and Lucassen, eds., *Migration, Migration History, History*, 257; Jane E. Mangan, *Transatlantic Obligations: Creating the Bonds of Family in Conquest-Era Peru and Spain* (Oxford: Oxford University Press, 2016), 98–119.

22. See James Lockhart and Enrique Otte, eds., *Letters and People of the Spanish Indies: Sixteenth Century* (Cambridge: Cambridge University Press, 1976); Enrique Otte, ed., *Cartas privadas de emigrantes a Indias 1540–1616* (Seville: Consejería de Cultura, Junta de Andalucía, Escuela de Estudios Hispano Americanos de Sevilla, 1988).

23. Otte, *Cartas privadas*, 240, as translated in Henry Kamen, *Empire: How Spain Became a World Power, 1492–1763* (New York: Harper Collins, 2003), 129.

24. Studies that concern the impact of emigration, transatlantic contact, and return migration on Spanish sending communities include Ida Altman, *Emigrants and Society: Extremadura and Spanish America in the Sixteenth Century* (Berkeley: University of California Press, 1989), and Juan Javier Pescador, *The New World inside a Basque Village: The Oiartzun Valley and Its*

Atlantic Emigrants, 1550–1800 (Reno and Las Vegas: University of Nevada Press, 2004). Carlos Alberto González Sánchez explores the family ties of ordinary Spaniards between Spain and Peru in *Dineros de ventura: La varia fortuna de la emigración a Indias (siglos XVI–XVII)* (Seville: Universidad de Sevilla, 1995). Also see Mangan, *Transatlantic Obligations*.

25. Lockhart and Schwartz, *Early Latin America*, 103–5, 324–25; Lockhart and Otte, *Letters and People*, 128.

26. Altman and Horn, introduction, in Altman and Horn, eds., *"To Make America"*, 5.

27. Ida Altman, *Transatlantic Ties in the Spanish Empire: Brihuega, Spain, and Puebla, Mexico, 1560–1620* (Stanford, CA: Stanford University Press, 2000).

28. Altman, "Spanish Women in the Caribbean," in Owens and Mangan, eds., *Women of the Iberian Atlantic*, 72–73; Lockhart, *The Men of Cajamarca*, 43–64.

29. The Extremaduran towns of Cáceres and Trujillo were so closely associated with Peru that a returnee was called a *perulero*, virtually eclipsing the use of the term *indiano*. See Altman, *Emigrants and Society*, 172, 339n2.

30. Mangan, *Transatlantic Obligations*, 70–97.

31. Altman, "Spanish Migration to the Americas," in Cohen, ed., *The Cambridge Survey of World Migration*, 31; and Altman, *Emigrants and Society*, 247–74. Also see Altman, *Transatlantic Ties in the Spanish Empire*, 37–39; Pescador, *The New World inside a Basque Village*.

32. Hoerder, *Cultures in Contact*, 193.

33. David Studnicki-Gizbert, *A Nation upon the Ocean Sea: Portugal's Atlantic Diaspora and the Crisis of the Spanish Empire, 1492–1640* (Oxford: Oxford University Press, 2007); David Wheat, *Atlantic Africa and the Spanish Caribbean, 1570–1640* (Chapel Hill: University of North Carolina Press, 2016), 17, 104–32, 268; Mörner, "Migraciones a Hispanoamérica," *Anuario de estudios americanos*, 9–10; Boyd-Bowman, "Patterns of Spanish Emigration," *HAHR*, 588; Kicza, "Patterns in Early Spanish Overseas Expansion," *WMQ*, 241–42; Lewis Hanke, "The Portuguese in Spanish America, with Special Reference to the Villa Imperial de Potosí," *Revista de historia de América* 51 (1958), 1–48; Woodrow Borah, "The Portuguese of Tulancingo and the Special *Donativo* of 1642–1643," *Jahrbuch für Geschichte von Staat, Wirtschaft und Gesellschaft Lateinamerikas* 4 (1967), 386–98; Mörner, "Spanish Migration to the New World prior to 1810," in Chiappelli, ed., *First Images of America*, 2:739–40; Kamen, *Empire*, 132–35; Sánchez-Albornoz, "The First Transatlantic Transfer," in Canny,

ed., *Europeans on the Move*, 29 and 35; Malyn Newitt, *Emigration and the Sea: An Alternative History of Portugal and the Portuguese* (Oxford: Oxford University Press, 2015), 40, 64–67; Robert J. Ferry, *The Colonial Elite of Early Caracas: Formation and Crisis, 1567–1767* (Berkeley: University of California Press, 1989). Included among the 350 Europeans who initially settled in Paraguay were Portuguese, Germans, and Italians; see Lockhart and Schwartz, *Early Latin America*, 259–60.

34. Hanke, "The Portuguese in Spanish America," *Revista de historia de América*, 10–12, 14–15.

35. Jonathan I. Israel, *Diasporas within a Diaspora: Jews, Crypto-Jews and the World Maritime Empires (1540–1740)* (Leiden: Brill, 2002), 18–19, 29–30, 97–150.

36. On the brazilwood trade, see Warren Dean, *With Broadax and Firebrand: Destruction of the Brazilian Atlantic Forest* (Berkeley: University of California Press, 1995); and Shawn William Miller, *Fruitless Trees: Portuguese Conservation and Brazil's Colonial Timber* (Stanford, CA: Stanford University Press, 2000).

37. On Portuguese immigration to Brazil, see Maria Luiza Marcílio, "The Population of Colonial Brazil," in *CHLA*, 2:42–52; Vitorino Magalhães Godinho, "Portuguese Expansion from the Fifteenth to the Twentieth Century: Constants and Changes," in P. C. Emmer and Magnus Mörner, eds., *European Expansion and Migration: Essays on Intercontinental Migration from Africa, Asia, and Europe* (New York and Oxford: Berg, 1992), 13–48; A. J. R. Russell-Wood, "Patterns of Settlement in the Portuguese Empire, 1400–1800," in Bethencourt and Curto, eds., *Portuguese Oceanic Expansion*, 161–96; A. J. R. Russell-Wood, *A World on the Move: The Portuguese in Africa, Asia, and America, 1415–1808* (New York: St. Martin's Press, 1993); Newitt, *Emigration and the Sea*, esp. 107–28; A. R. Disney, *A History of Portugal and the Portuguese Empire*, vol. 2, *The Portuguese Empire* (Cambridge: Cambridge University Press, 2009), 211, 214. For *degredados* and orphans of the king, see Timothy J. Coates, *Convicts and Orphans: Forced and State-Sponsored Colonizers in the Portuguese Empire, 1550–1755* (Stanford, CA: Stanford University Press, 2001); Disney, *A History of Portugal*, 2:206–7, 211, 213. For the rise of the sugar industry in Brazil, see Stuart B. Schwartz, *Sugar Plantations in the Formation of Brazilian Society: Bahia, 1550–1835* (Cambridge: Cambridge University Press, 1985).

38. David Eltis, "The Volume and Structure of the Transatlantic Slave Trade: A Reassessment," *WMQ* 58 (2001), table 3, p. 45.

39. Kamen, *Empire*, 133–34.

40. Russell-Wood, "Patterns of Settlement," in Bethencourt and Curto, eds., *Portuguese Oceanic Expansion*, 175. For a bibliography on Portuguese emigration, see Edward A. Alpers and Molly Ball, "'Portuguese Diasporas': A Survey of the Scholarly Literature," in Eric Morier-Genoud and Michel Cahen, eds., *Imperial Migrations: Colonial Communities and Diaspora in the Portuguese World* (New York: Palgrave Macmillan, 2012), 31–71.

41. For regional origins, see H. B. Johnson, "The Portuguese Settlement of Brazil, 1500–1580," in *CHLA*, 1:283; Studnicki-Gizbert, *A Nation upon the Ocean Sea*, 48–55.

42. Newitt, *Emigration and the* Sea, 26–30. Also see A. R. Disney, *A History of Portugal*, vol. 1, *Portugal* (Cambridge: Cambridge University Press, 2009), 145–46.

43. Victor Pereira Rosa and Salvato Trigo, *Azorean Emigration: A Preliminary Overview* (Porto: Fernando Pessoa University Press, 1994).

44. Newitt, *Emigration and the Sea*, 36, 110–11; Disney, *A History of Portugal*, 2:237, 245, 254, 294; Alida C. Metcalf, *Go-Betweens and the Colonization of Brazil, 1500–1600* (Austin: University of Texas Press, 2005), 38. Many soldiers conscripted in Portugal never returned from Brazil, due to either death, desertion, or the decision to remain in Brazil after being discharged. See C. R. Boxer, *The Golden Age of Brazil: Growing Pains of a Colonial Society, 1695–1750* (New York: St. Martin's Press, 1995; orig. pub. 1962), 141–43.

45. Susan Migden Socolow, *The Women of Colonial Latin America*, 2nd ed (New York: Cambridge University Press, 2015), 64; Russell-Wood, "Patterns of Settlement," in Bethencourt and Curto, eds., *Portuguese Oceanic Expansion*, quotation: 172.

46. Unlike Spain, which (in 1492) expelled Jews unwilling to convert, Portugal forced its entire Jewish population—approximately 190,000 people, or nearly 20 percent of the population—to convert. The first generation of New Christians (or *conversos*) included many secretly practicing Jews. They and their descendants were treated with suspicion by Portuguese Catholics and were also subjected to the Inquisition after it was established in the 1540s. Many New Christians thus fled to the relative safety of Brazil, where the Inquisition was never formally established, though individuals at times were given inquisitorial powers. See Arnold Wiznitzer, *Jews in Colonial Brazil* (New York: Columbia University Press, 1960). Emigration apparently increased while New Christians were being actively persecuted and stopped in the 1760s, when reforms ended their legal persecution in Portugal. See Newitt, *Emigration and the Sea*, 66–67, 73.

47. See Wiznitzer, *Jews in Colonial Brazil*; and Marcílio, "The Population of Colonial Brazil," in *CHLA*, 2:46. According to the provisions of the Treaty of Utrecht (1579), which united the seven northern provinces of the Netherlands, "no one within the territory of the Dutch republic could be persecuted for his religious convictions or practices." See Wiznitzer, *Jews in Colonial Brazil*, 43.

48. Marcílio, "The Population of Colonial Brazil," in *CHLA*, 2:46. On the Dutch occupation of Brazil, see Leonardo Dantas Silva, *Holandeses em Pernambuco, 1630–1654* (Recife, Brazil: Instituto Richard Brennand, 2005); C. R. Boxer, *The Dutch in Brazil, 1624–1654* (Oxford: Clarendon Press, 1957); Disney, *A History of Portugal*, 2:221–31.

49. See Bruno Feitler, "Jews and New Christians in Dutch Brazil, 1630–1654," in Richard L. Kagan and Philip D. Morgan, *Atlantic Diasporas: Jews, Conversos, and Crypto-Jews in the Age of Mercantilism, 1500–1800* (Baltimore: Johns Hopkins University Press, 2009), 123–51.

50. Hanke, "The Portuguese in Spanish America," *Revista de historia de América*, 4–5; Richard M. Morse, ed., *Bandeirantes: The Historical Role of the Brazilian Pathfinders* (New York: Alfred A. Knopf, 1965), 11, 15, 16.

51. Richard S. Dunn, *Sugar and Slaves: The Rise of the Planter Class in the English West Indies, 1624–1713* (Chapel Hill: University of North Carolina Press, 1972), 3–45.

52. On the comparative history of indentured servitude, see P. C. Emmer, ed., *Colonialism and Migration: Indentured Labour before and after Slavery* (Dordrecht: Martinus Nijhoff, 1986); and Charles Bergquist, "The Paradox of American Development," in *Labor and the Course of American Democracy: US History in Latin American Perspective* (New York and London: Verso, 1996).

53. See E. van den Boogaart and P. C. Emmer, "Colonialism and Migration," in Emmer, ed., *Colonialism and Migration*, 3.

54. On indentured servitude in Barbados, see Simon P. Newman, *A New World of Labor: The Development of Plantation Slavery in the British Atlantic* (Philadelphia: University of Pennsylvania Press, 2013), 54–107; in the Chesapeake, see James Horn, "Servant Emigration to the Chesapeake in the Seventeenth Century," in Thad Tate and David Ammerman, eds., *The Chesapeake in the Seventeenth Century: Essays on Anglo-American Society* (Chapel Hill: University of North Carolina Press, 1979), 51–95, and Russell R. Menard, "British Migration to the Chesapeake Colonies in the Seventeenth Century," in Lois Green Carr, Philip D. Morgan, and Jean B. Russo, eds., *Colonial Chesapeake Society* (Chapel Hill: University of North Carolina Press, 1988), 99–132.

55. Dunn, *Sugar and Slaves*, 49–59, 164–65; John J. McCusker and Russell R. Menard, "The Sugar Industry in the Seventeenth Century: A New Perspective on the Barbadian 'Sugar Revolution,'" in Stuart B. Schwartz, ed., *Tropical Babylons: Sugar and the Making of the Atlantic World, 1450–1680* (Chapel Hill: University of North Carolina Press, 2004), 289–330.

56. Newman, *A New World of Labor*, 61–64, 71–75.

57. Edmund Morgan, *American Slavery, American Freedom: The Ordeal of Colonial Virginia* (New York: Norton, 1975), 90 and following; T. H. Breen, *Tobacco Culture: The Mentality of the Great Tidewater Planters on the Eve of Revolution* (Princeton, NJ: Princeton University Press, 1985), 46–55.

58. Alison Games, *Migration and the Origins of the English Atlantic World* (Cambridge, MA: Harvard University Press, 1999), 16; Bernard Bailyn, *The Peopling of British North America: An Introduction* (New York: Knopf, 1986), 20–43, quotation: 25. In 1635 alone, nearly 5,000 emigrants departed from London for American destinations, including just over 2,000 sailing for the Chesapeake and another 1,700 bound for the Caribbean; see Games, *Migration and the Origins of the English Atlantic,* table 1.1, p. 21.

59. See Abbot Emerson Smith, *Colonists in Bondage: White Servitude and Convict Labor in America, 1607–1776* (Chapel Hill: University of North Carolina Press, 1947); and David W. Galenson, *White Servitude in Colonial America: An Economic Analysis* (Cambridge: Cambridge University Press, 1981).

60. Before the mid-seventeenth century, Scots went in significant numbers to Ireland as farmers; to Europe (especially Poland) as merchants, peddlers, tradesmen, and soldiers; to Scandinavia as traders and especially soldiers; and to England, finding diverse employment. Scholars estimate that between 1600 and 1650, between a minimum of 85,000 and a maximum of 115,000 Scots emigrated, most of them young men. Smout et al., "Scottish Emigration," in Canny, ed., *Europeans on the Move*, 76–86.

61. Menard, "British Migration to the Chesapeake Colonies in the Seventeenth Century," in Carr et al., eds., *Colonial Chesapeake Society*, 99–132; Canny, "English Migration," in Canny, ed., *Europeans on the Move*, 50. For a detailed portrait of one Maryland planter prior to the transition to slavery, see Lois Green Carr, Russell R. Menard, and Lorena S. Walsh, *Robert Cole's World: Agriculture and Society in Early Maryland* (Chapel Hill: University of North Carolina Press, 1991).

62. James Horn, "'To Parts beyond the Seas': Free Emigration to the Chesapeake in the Seventeenth Century," in Altman and Horn, eds., *"To Make America"*, 109.

63. Horn, "'To Parts beyond the Seas,'" in Altman and Horn, eds., *To Make America*", 87; Lois Green Carr and Russell R. Menard, "Immigration and Opportunity: The Freedman in Colonial Maryland," in Tate and Ammerman, eds., *The Chesapeake in the Seventeenth Century*, 206–42. For a focused analysis of the 1635 London emigrant cohort, see Games, *Migration and the Origins of the English Atlantic*, 105–14.

64. On the free European population of the Chesapeake, see Horn, "'To Parts beyond the Seas,'" in Altman and Horn, eds., *"To Make America"*; on the impact of the headright system, see especially Anthony S. Parent Jr., *Foul Means: The Formation of a Slave Society in Virginia, 1660–1740* (Chapel Hill: University of North Carolina Press, 2003), 25–29, 40–47.

65. In the Chesapeake, the Jamestown site was especially unhealthful; see Carville V. Earle, "Environment, Disease, and Mortality in Early Virginia," in Tate and Ammerman, eds., *The Chesapeake in the Seventeenth Century*, 96–125. For Middlesex County, see Darrett B. Rutman and Anita H. Rutman, "'Now-Wives and Sons-in-Law': Parental Death in a Seventeenth-Century County," in Tate and Ammerman, eds., *The Chesapeake in the Seventeenth Century*, 153–182; and Darrett B. Rutman and Anita H. Rutman, *A Place in Time: Explicatus* (New York: Norton, 1984), 37–59, 79–81. For Maryland, see especially Lois Green Carr and Lorena S. Walsh, "The Planter's Wife: The Experience of White Women in Seventeenth-Century Maryland," *WMQ* 34 (1977), 542–71, and Gloria Lund Main, *Tobacco Colony: Life in Early Maryland, 1650–1720* (Princeton, NJ: Princeton University Press, 1982), 15.

66. On Dutch emigration, see Lucassen, "The Netherlands, the Dutch, and Long-Distance Migration," in Canny, ed., *Europeans on the Move*, 153–91; and "No Golden Age Without Migration? The Case of the Dutch Republic in a Comparative Perspective," in Simonetta Cavaciocchi, ed., *Le migrazioni in Europa: secc. XIII–XVIII* (Prato, Italy: Istituto Internazionale di Storia Economica "F. Datini," 1994), 775–97; and Ernst van den Boogaart, "The Servant Migration to New Netherland, 1624–1664," in Emmer, ed., *Colonialism and Migration*, 55–75. For a comparison with Portugal, see Canny, "In Search of a Better Home?," in Canny, ed., *Europeans on the Move*, 270–72.

67. Lucassen, "The Netherlands, the Dutch, and Long-Distance Migration," in Canny, ed., *Europeans on the Move*, 173–80; van den Boogaart, "The Servant Migration to New Netherland," in Emmer, ed., *Colonialism and Migration*, 57–59; Bernard Bailyn, "Introduction: Europeans on the Move, 1500–1800," in Canny, ed., *Europeans on the Move*, 2.

68. On French immigration to the Americas, see Yves Landry, "Les français passes au Canada avant 1760: Le regard de l'émigrant," *Revue*

d'histoire de l'Amérique française, 59 (2006), 481–500; Christian Huetz de Lemps, "Indentured Servants Bound for the French Antilles in the Seventeenth and Eighteenth Centuries," in Altman and Horn, eds., *To Make America*", 172–203; Frédéric Mauro, "French Indentured Servants for America, 1500–1800," in Emmer, ed., *Colonialism and Migration*, 83–104; Peter N. Moogk, "Reluctant Exiles: Emigrants from France in Canada before 1760," *WMQ* 46 (1989), 463–505; Peter Moogk, "Manon's Fellow Exiles: Emigration from France to North America before 1763," in Canny, ed., *Europeans on the Move*, 236–60; Leslie Choquette, "Recruitment of French Emigrants to Canada, 1600–1760," in Altman and Horn, eds., *"To Make America"*, 131–71; Leslie Choquette, *Frenchmen into Peasants: Modernity and Tradition in the Peopling of French Canada* (Cambridge, MA: Harvard University Press, 1997); J. M. Bumsted, *The Peoples of Canada: A Pre-Confederation History* (Oxford: Oxford University Press, 2003), 118–24; Allan Greer, *The People of New France* (Toronto: University of Toronto Press, 1997), 11–26.

The most widely accepted estimate for immigration to Canada comes from Mario Boleda, who argues for 33,500 French emigrants by 1760; see Boleda, "Nouvelle estimation de l'immigration française au Canada, 1608–1760," in Yves Landry, ed., *Le peuplement du Canada aux XVIIe et XVIIIe siècles: Actes des premières journées d'étude du Programme de Recherche sur l'Émigration des Français en Nouvelle-France (PRÉFEN)* (Caen: Universitéde Caen Basse-Normandie, 2004), 29–37. Boleda has been concerned primarily with identifying founding migrants, or migrants who remained in Canada. Estimating a return migration rate of 70 percent, Choquette contends that, when temporary migrants are accounted for, some 67,000 French men and women migrated to Canada; see *Frenchmen into Peasants*, 21.

Some estimates of the number of French emigrants to American colonies are as low as 50,000–60,000; see, e.g., Altman and Horn, introduction, in Altman and Horn, eds., *"To Make America"*, 4; Engerman and Sokoloff, "Factor Endowments," in Haber, ed., *How Latin America Fell Behind*, 264; and Canny, "In Search of a Better Home?," in Canny, ed., *Europeans on the Move*, 276. Other scholars offer a broader range, with a high end around 100,000; see, for example, James Pritchard, *In Search of Empire: The French in the Americas, 1670–1730* (New York: Cambridge University Press, 2004), 17, who argues that it is "highly unlikely" that emigration reached 100,000; David Eltis, *The Rise of African Slavery in the Americas* (Cambridge: Cambridge University Press, 2000), 9, table 1-1, which offers an estimate of 100,000; and, following Eltis, Philip P. Boucher, *France and the American Tropics to 1700: Tropics of Discontent?* (Baltimore: Johns Hopkins University

Press, 2008), 10, which presents an estimated range of 60,000–100,000. Because we believe that migration to the French Caribbean has likely been underestimated (see the next paragraph and n. 69, below), we have selected the high end of this range—100,000—for inclusion in Table 1. For soldiers' persistence, see Pritchard, *In Search of Empire*, 22.

69. Jean Tanguy, "Les engagés nantais pour les Antilles," *Actes du 97e congrès national des sociétés savants* (Nantes, 1972), 53–54; Boucher, *France and the American Tropics to 1700*, 144–46 and following; Gabriel Debien, "Les engagés pour les Antilles, 1634–1715," *Revue d'histoire des colonies* 38 (1951), "Tableau général des départs (1638–1715)," 248–49; Pritchard, *In Search of Empire*, 43–71, and appendix 1, "Estimated Population of French America by Race and Region, 1670–1730," 423–27.

70. Pritchard, *In Search of Empire*, 23; Debien, "Les engagés pour les Antilles," *Revue d'histoire des colonies*, 141–42. See also Huetz de Lemps, "Indentured Servants," in Altman and Horn, eds., *"To Make America"*; and Mauro, "French Indentured Servants," in Emmer, ed., *Colonialism and Migration*. Moogk estimates a total of not more than 37,000 indentured servants to French America, the majority going to the Caribbean; see Moogk, "Manon's Fellow Exiles," in Canny, ed., *Europeans on the Move*, 252.

71. Greer, *The People of New France*, 15. One study concerning indentured servants embarking in La Rochelle in the eighteenth century indicates that many of the young men "had lost at least one parent, and often they are listed as orphans." Yet it also highlights the significance of family or hometown ties: "they frequently left their villages in twos (sometimes from the same family), brothers or cousins, or with the same trade, perhaps working together)." See Huetz de Lemps, "Indentured Servants," in Altman and Horn, eds., *"To Make America"*, quotations: 198.

72. See Huetz de Lemps, "Indentured Servants," in Altman and Horn, eds., *"To Make America"*, 188–89; Mauro, "French Indentured Servants," in Emmer, ed., *Colonialism and Migration*, 97–100.

73. Huetz de Lemps, "Indentured Servants," in Altman and Horn, eds., *"To Make America"*, 175.

74. Alfred W. Crosby, *Ecological Imperialism: The Biological Expansion of Europe, 900–1900* (New York: Cambridge University Press, 1986), 2–3 and following.

75. The seigneurial system of New France has been the subject of extensive debate; see especially Richard Colebrook Harris, *The Seigneurial System in Early Canada: A Geographical Study* (Madison: University of Wisconsin

Press, 1968); Louise Dechêne, *Habitants and Merchants in Seventeenth Century Montreal*, trans. Liana Vardi (Montreal and Kingston, Ont.: McGill–Queen's University Press, 1992; orig. pub. France, 1974), 134–43; Winstanley Briggs, "Le Pays de Illinois," *WMQ* 47 (1990), 30–56; W. J. Eccles, *The French in North America, 1500–1783*, rev. ed. (East Lansing: Michigan State University Press, 1998), 38–40 and following; and Greer, *The People of New France*, 36–40. For New England, see especially David Grayson Allen, *In English Ways: The Movement of Societies and the Transferal of English Local Law and Custom to Massachusetts Bay in the Seventeenth Century* (Chapel Hill: University of North Carolina Press, 1981).

76. Virginia DeJohn Anderson, *New England's Generation: The Great Migration and the Formation of Society and Culture in the Seventeenth Century* (New York: Cambridge University Press, 1991); Games, *Migration and the Origins of the English Atlantic*, 132–62.

77. John Murrin, "Beneficiaries of Catastrophe: The English Colonies in America," in Eric Foner, ed., *The New American History* (Philadelphia: Temple University Press, 1990), 11–12; Boleda, "Nouvelle estimation," in Landry, ed., *Le peuplement du Canada*, 37.

78. Joyce D. Goodfriend, *Before the Melting Pot: Society and Culture in Colonial New York City, 1664–1730* (Princeton, NJ: Princeton University Press, 1992); Ned Landsman, *Scotland and Its First American Colony, 1683–1760* (Princeton, NJ: Princeton University Press, 1985); James T. Lemon, *The Best Poor Man's Country: A Geographical Study of Early Southeastern Pennsylvania* (Baltimore: Johns Hopkins University Press, 1972), quotation: xiii.

79. Sánchez-Albornoz, "The First Transatlantic Transfer," in Canny, ed., *Europeans on the Move*, 32–33. Carlos Martínez Shaw has revised estimates for Spanish emigration dramatically downward from the 688,000 presented in this essay (see Table 1) by almost 40 percent, to a total of 475,000 emigrants. For the sixteenth century, he accepts the figure of 243,000 proposed by Mörner. For the seventeenth century, for which information is much scarcer, Martínez Shaw synthesizes and extrapolates from various regional, provincial, and local studies in Spain to arrive at a total of just 100,000—far fewer emigrants than the 190,000 proposed by Mörner for just the first half of the century, based on an analysis of transatlantic shipping records. Relying in part on the important work of Rosario Márquez Macías, Martínez Shaw estimates an additional 125,000 emigrants from 1700 to 1824. See Carlos Martínez Shaw, *La emigración española a América (1492–1824)* (Asturias, Spain: Fundación Archivo de Indianos, 1994); for Márquez Macías, see "La emigración española a

América (1765–1824)" (PhD dissertation, Universidad de Oviedo, 1994).
We have chosen to rely on Mörner rather than Martínez Shaw, primarily
because the higher estimates Mörner presents have been widely accepted
in the literature and his method rests on the use of transatlantic shipping
records. However, it is important to note that the disagreement between
them highlights the incompleteness of early modern data and, consequently,
the provisional nature of these estimates.

80. Alan Knight, *Mexico: The Colonial Era* (New York: Cambridge
University Press, 2002), 182.

81. On the rise of Atlantic communications in the eighteenth-century
British Atlantic, see Ian K. Steele, *The English Atlantic, 1675–1740: An
Exploration of Communication and Community* (New York: Oxford
University Press, 1986); on eighteenth-century Atlantic trade, see David
Hancock, *Citizens of the World: London Merchants and the Integration of
the British Atlantic Community* (New York: Cambridge University Press,
1995), and David Hancock, *Oceans of Wine: Madeira and the Emergence of
American Trade and Taste* (New Haven, CT: Yale University Press, 2009);
on migration to the eighteenth-century British colonies, see Bailyn, *The
Peopling of British North America*, Bernard Bailyn, *Voyagers to the West:
A Passage in the Peopling of America on the Eve of Revolution* (New York:
Knopf, 1986), Marianne S. Wokeck, *Trade in Strangers: The Beginnings of
Mass Migration to North America* (University Park: Penn State University
Press, 1999), and A. Roger Ekirch, *Bound for America: The Transportation of
British Convicts to the Colonies, 1718–1775* (New York: Oxford University
Press, 1990). For the eighteenth-century Spanish Atlantic, see Jeremy
Baskes, *Staying Afloat: Risk and Uncertainty in Spanish Atlantic World Trade,
1760–1820* (Stanford, CA: Stanford University Press, 2013), and Kenneth
J. Andrien, "The Spanish Atlantic System," in Jack P. Greene and Philip
D. Morgan, eds., *Atlantic History: A Critical Appraisal* (New York: Oxford
University Press, 2009), 55–79. Also see the essays in Nicholas Canny and
Philip Morgan, eds., *The Oxford Handbook of the Atlantic World, 1450–1850*
(Oxford: Oxford University Press, 2011).

82. The central role African slavery played in eighteenth-century
economic development was explored most famously by Eric Williams,
Capitalism and Slavery (Chapel Hill: University of North Carolina Press,
1994; orig. pub. 1944); see also Sidney W. Mintz, *Sweetness and Power: The
Place of Sugar in Modern History* (New York: Viking, 1985); and Eltis, *Rise
of African Slavery in the Americas.*

83. Peter Bakewell, *A History of Latin America to 1825*, 3rd ed. (Malden,
MA: Wiley-Blackwell, 2010), 351–364; Sánchez-Albornoz, "The First

Transatlantic Transfer," in Canny, ed., *Europeans on the Move*, 32–36, and John Kicza, "The Social and Political Position of Spanish Immigration in Bourbon America and the Origins of the Independence Movements," *Colonial Latin American Review* 4:1 (1995), 105–28.

84. No more than 15 percent of the immigrants resident in New Spain in 1742 were women; see Charles F. Nunn, *Foreign Immigrants in Early Bourbon Mexico, 1700–1760* (Cambridge: Cambridge University Press, 1979), 4.

85. D. A. Brading, *Miners and Merchants in Bourbon Mexico, 1763–1810* (Cambridge: Cambridge University Press, 1971); Susan Migden Socolow, *The Merchants of Buenos Aires, 1778–1810: Family and Commerce* (Cambridge: Cambridge University Press, 1978).

86. Sherry Johnson, *The Social Transformation of Eighteenth-Century Cuba* (Gainesville: University Press of Florida, 2001); Ruth Pike, *Penal Servitude in Early Modern Spain* (Madison: University of Wisconsin Press, 1983), 134–47; Sánchez-Albornoz, "The First Transatlantic Transfer," in Canny, ed., *Europeans on the Move*, 33; Juan Marchena Fernández, *Oficiales y soldados en el ejército de América* (Seville: Escuela de Estudios Hispanos-Americanos, Universidad de Sevilla, 1983), 56–58.

87. Parsons, "The Migration of Canary Islanders to the Americas," *The Americas*, 460–64. Recent studies include Allyson Poska, *Gendered Crossings: Women and Migration in the Spanish Empire* (Albuquerque: University of New Mexico Press, 2016); Juan Manuel Santana Pérez and José Antonio Sánchez Suárez, "Repoblación de Costa de Mosquitos en el ultimo cuarto del siglo XVIII," *Revista de Indias* 67:241 (2007), 695–712; Nadia Andrea de Cristóforis, "Ideas y políticas migratorias españolas a fines del Antiguo Régimen: El caso astur-galaico," *Anuario de estudios americanos* 63 (2006), 117–50; David J. Weber, *The Spanish Frontier in North America* (New Haven, CT: Yale University Press, 1992), 192–94.

88. Marcílio, "The Population of Colonial Brazil," in *CHLA*, 2:48; Disney, *A History of Portugal*, 2:270–72. For population pressure in the Azores in the eighteenth century, see Newitt, *Emigration and the Sea*, 44.

89. Russell-Wood, "Patterns of Settlement," in Bethencourt and Curto, eds., *Portuguese Oceanic Expansion*, 164, 175.

90. Marcílio, "The Population of Colonial Brazil," in *CHLA*, 2:47–48. Also see Russell-Wood, *A World on the Move*, 59, 61. Newitt asserts that between 500,000 and 600,000 Portuguese arrived in Brazil in the first half of the eighteenth century; see *Emigration and the Sea*, 115.

91. Estimates vary from 10,000 to 20,000 people. See Newitt, *Emigration and the Sea*, 119; Disney, *A History of Portugal*, 1:331; Mark A. Burkholder

and Lyman L. Johnson, *Colonial Latin America,* 7th ed. (New York: Oxford University Press, 2010), 363.

92. On French efforts in Brazil, see John Hemming, *Red Gold: The Conquest of the Brazilian Indians, 1500–1760* (Cambridge, MA: Harvard University Press, 1978), 8–9, 12, 118; Olive Patricia Dickason, "The Sixteenth-Century French Vision of Empire: The Other Side of Self-Determination," in Germaine Warkentin and Carolyn Podruchny, eds., *Decentering the Renaissances: Canada and Europe in Multidisciplinary Perspective, 1500–1700* (Toronto: University of Toronto Press, 2001), 87–109; and Silvia Castro Shannon, "Military Outpost or Protestant Refuge: Villegagnon's Expedition to Brazil in 1555," in Andrew John Bayly Johnston, ed., *Essays in French Colonial History,* Proceedings of the 21st Annual Meeting of the French Colonial Society (Lansing: Michigan State University Press, 1997), 1–13.

93. Marcílio, "The Population of Colonial Brazil," in *CHLA,* 2:46, 48–49, quotation: 49; Russell-Wood, "Patterns of Settlement," in Bethencourt and Curto, eds., *Portuguese Oceanic Expansion,* 174; Russell-Wood, *A World on the Move,* 62; Newitt, *Emigration and the Sea,* 35; Disney, *A History of Portugal,* 2:293. The Portuguese crown also deported Romanies (*ciganos*) to Brazil in the eighteenth century, continuing a pattern that began earlier; see Bill M. Donovan, "Changing Perceptions of Social Deviance: Gypsies in Early Modern Portugal and Brazil," *Journal of Social History* 26:1 (1992), 33–53.

94. Patrick Griffin, *The People with No Name: Ireland's Ulster Scots, America's Scots Irish, and the Creation of a British Atlantic World, 1689–1764* (Princeton, NJ: Princeton University Press, 2001); see also James G. Leyburn, *The Scotch-Irish: A Social History* (Chapel Hill: University of North Carolina Press, 1962).

95. Bailyn, *The Peopling of British North America,* 16; Fogleman, *Hopeful Journeys,* table I.1, p. 2, and 179n12; Eric Hinderaker and Peter C. Mancall, *At the Edge of Empire: The Backcountry in British North America* (Baltimore: Johns Hopkins University Press, 2003).

96. Bailyn, *Voyagers to the West,* 126–352; Ekirch, *Bound for America,* 21–27, 124–25, 133–93. For an engaging account of one indentured servant's experience, see William Moraley, *The Infortunate: The Voyage and Adventures of William Moraley, an Indentured Servant,* ed. Susan E. Klepp and Billy G. Smith, 2nd ed. (University Park: Penn State University Press, 2005).

97. Bailyn, *Voyagers to the West,* 126–239, 355–637.

98. Huetz de Lemps, "Indentured Servants," in Altman and Horn, eds., *"To Make America"*, 173, 183–87, 191, quotation: 199. In 1699, the crown also obliged each planter to have one indentured servant to every twenty African slaves. On crown requirements to transport indentured servants, also see Moogk, "Manon's Fellow Exiles," in Canny, ed., *Europeans on the Move*, 245–46.

99. Huetz de Lemps, "Indentured Servants," in Altman and Horn, eds., *"To Make America"*, 182; Moogk, "Reluctant Exiles," *WMQ*, 503; Moogk, "Manon's Fellow Exiles," in Canny, ed., *Europeans on the Move*, 256–57; Carl A. Brasseaux, "The Image of Louisiana and the Failure of Voluntary French Emigration, 1683–1731," in Alf Heggoy and James J. Cooke, eds., *Proceedings of the Fourth Meeting of the French Colonial Historical Society* (Washington, DC: University Press of America, 1979), 47–56; James J. Cooke, "France, the New World, and Colonial Expansion," in Patricia K. Galloway, ed., *La Salle and His Legacy: Frenchmen and Indians in the Lower Mississippi Valley* (Jackson: University of Mississippi Press, 1982), 81–92; Daniel J. Usner, *Indians, Settlers, and Slaves in a Frontier Exchange Economy: The Lower Mississippi Valley before 1783* (Chapel Hill: University of North Carolina Press, 1992), 24–25, 31–33, 46–51, 108; Greer, *The People of New France*, 105–6. Bumsted, *The Peoples of Canada*, quotation: 118. Moogk notes: "Self-financed, independent newcomers were so rare in New France that they were noted in administrative records and in official correspondence"; "Reluctant Exiles," *WMQ*, 473.

100. Christopher Hodson, *The Acadian Diaspora: An Eighteenth-Century History* (New York: Oxford University Press, 2012); Emma Rothschild, "A Horrible Tragedy in the French Atlantic," *Past and Present* 192 (2006), 67–108, quotation: 71.